JAMES MCNAIR's
BURGERS

Photography and Styling by James McNair

Chronicle Books • San Francisco

Printed in Hong Kong

Library of Congress
Cataloging-in-Publication Data
McNair, James K.
[burgers]
James McNair's burgers/
photography and styling by James McNair
p. cm.
Includes indexes.
ISBN 0-8118-0098-9: $19.95
ISBN 0-8118-0093-8 (pbk.): $11.95
1. Cookery (Beef)
I. Title
TX749.5.B43M38 1992
641.6'62—dc20   92-10869
                          CIP

Distributed in Canada by
Raincoast Books
112 East Third Avenue
Vancouver, British Columbia V5T 1C8

10 9 8 7 6 5 4 3 2 1

Chronicle Books
275 Fifth Street
San Francisco, California 94103

For Andrew Moore, whom I met over a burger, and who brought music into my life when the world seemed too quiet and delivered joy in the midst of winter.

And in memory of Addie Prey, who sat on my lap while I typed the final words in this book, then died in my arms only two days later. Those readers who have followed this book series have seen credits to her as my loyal "secretary" and taste-tester through the years. For eighteen summers my beloved red tabby cat and I shared sunshine and burgers.

Produced by The Rockpile Press, San Francisco, Lake Tahoe, and the Napa Valley

Art direction, prop and food styling, and book design by James McNair

Kitchen and photographic assistance by Andrew Moore

Typography and mechanical production by Cleve Gallat of CTA Graphics

CONTENTS

BURGER BASICS   5

FAVORITE STANDARDS   11

AWARD WINNERS   31

CHEF SPECIALS   57

ACCOMPANIMENTS   85

INDEX   94

ACKNOWLEDGMENTS   96

BURGER BASICS

This book was a labor of love. If faced with the choice of a last meal, a perfect hamburger would certainly be on my short list. Meanwhile, I crave my weekly burger feast.

I've been a burger fancier all of my life. My early fascination with this all-American fare had simple roots. My best friend in childhood, John Louis LaPrairie, and I spent many hours in the kitchen of Bill's Cafe, his father's restaurant in Jonesville, Louisiana, watching Mary Jane prepare our lunch of hamburgers. Mine had to be plain—a well-done patty on a bun that was steamed on top of the panfrying meat, then spread with mayonnaise or, more likely, Miracle Whip.

All through my youth, much to the frustration of my daddy, whenever the family would go out to dine, a hamburger remained my menu choice.

Over the years my taste in condiments changed. I finally allowed Minnie and Shorty at the Homemade Drive-In to add cheese and tomato to my burger. And I learned to love mustards and onions. But in spite of my many years in California, I still believe that full-grown lettuce leaves and sprouts will ruin my burger. I do, however, like a few tender, young greens nestled against the garlic-accented mayonnaise that I enjoy today. And tomato slices must come from vine-ripened fruits, and not from those insipid, plastic-tasting ones found in too many markets.

Since burgers remain among my favorite foods, I was thrilled to serve as a judge for the first two Build A Better Burger national cookoffs. Held at the Sutter Home Winery in St. Helena, California, the cookoff gathers state and regional winners to the Napa Valley to grill up their original burgers. During my sojourn in the valley for the last cookoff, I began the search that led to the property that has since become my home, an idyllic spot overlooking the vineyards that surround the charming town of St. Helena. My new sylvan life owes its existence to a burger! And to a lost dog, but that is another book.

In addition to sharing my favorite ways of preparing hamburgers, this little volume contains award-winning recipes from the Sutter Home–sponsored cookoff and a grand collection of burgers shared by America's leading chefs.

ORIGIN

Cooked beef patties sandwiched between buns were introduced to the American public during the 1904 St. Louis International Exposition. They were served by German settlers of south St. Louis who named the sandwich in honor of their hometown of Hamburg. Residents of that German seaport had long favored beef that was minced and served on bread.

Grinding

I define a burger as a patty formed from some type of ground foodstuff that is cooked and served on or between a bread product.

To most people a burger means only ground beef. Today the United States Department of Agriculture requires that all beef labeled hamburger contain no more than 30 percent fat. Most markets offer a selection of ground beef based on its fat content. Ground sirloin, for example, contains only about 15 percent fat, and some markets carry a new type of lean beef that is as little as 10 percent fat.

Keep in mind, however, that great burgers can be made from ground veal, venison, sausage, turkey, chicken, and other meats, as well as fish, tofu, and vegetables. Very lean meats make better burgers when ground with a little fat to keep the meat moist and flavorful.

Since ground meat dries out quickly, many chefs and fine home cooks prefer to purchase a large cut of boneless meat and grind it shortly before cooking. Meat that is ground twice renders a burger that is more compact than that produced from a single grinding. This denser texture appeals to some burger connoisseurs. Others argue against grinding altogether and prefer to mince meat by hand with a cleaver or a chef's knife.

Storing

To store ground meat, form it into a mass no more than two inches thick. Wrap in butcher paper or plastic wrap and store the ground meat in the coldest part of the refrigerator for no longer than 24 hours.

If you must freeze burger patties, arrange uncooked patties in a single layer on open trays, and place in the freezer until firm, about 30 minutes. Once the patties are firm, stack them with squares of waxed paper in between. Wrap tightly in plastic wrap or place the stack of patties in a plastic freezer bag and return the patties to the freezer. Use within three months.

Preparing

Whether you stick with basic salt and pepper or add exotic spices, burgers will be more flavorful if the seasonings are mixed into the meat or other ground product before forming it into patties. Meat that has been ground for more than a few hours will cook up to a juicier finish if you work about two tablespoons beef or chicken stock into each pound of meat before forming it into patties. Nonbeef patties such as lean poultry, fish, or nuts may need a beaten egg, shredded cheese, or moistened bread crumbs to help bind them and keep them from falling apart during cooking. Patties made from low-fat meats or bland foodstuffs may need extra seasoning to make them flavorful.

Some cooks choose to stretch ground meat to cut down on the amount of fat consumed, to extend their budget, or just for the flavor. Consider adding one or more of the following per pound of meat: ½ cup fine fresh bread crumbs; ¼ cup ground nuts, dry cereal, wheat germ, ground seeds, or presoaked bulgur; ½ cup finely grated carrot or potato; or ½ cup finely minced fresh mushrooms or bean sprouts.

When adding seasonings and shaping into patties, always handle ground meat or other mixtures as little as possible to avoid compacting them; gentle handling keeps the texture light. For even cooking, make all the patties the same size by dividing the ground meat or other burger mixture into equal portions. Using your hands, form each portion into a round, oval, square, or rectangle about the same size and shape as the bread on which it will be served. Form neat edges with your fingertips, but remember not to press too hard and compact the meat. Please do not use that ridiculous gadget, the hamburger press, that compresses the meat into perfect flat disks. If the burgers are to be grilled, keep the patties thick (from ¾ to 1 inch) so that the interiors remain juicy and moist while the surface chars. Patties that will be broiled or pancooked may be a bit thinner.

I cringe when I read directions, sometimes even from otherwise reliable sources, that instruct cooks to press down on the patties while they are cooking. On a grill or under a broiler, that means that all the delicious juices are lost through the grill rack, plus the drips cause flare-ups that will overchar the burgers. On a grill, under a broiler, or in a skillet, pressing out the juices compacts the meat and makes it tough and dry.

No matter which method of cooking you choose, please never press down on a hamburger patty.

TIMING

Cooking times vary with the type of grill, broiler, or pan used; whether burgers are cooked uncovered or covered when grilling; position of the grill heat source—*i.e.*, directly under the patties versus offset from the patties; temperature of cooking surface; thickness and internal temperature of the patties; and, of course, individual preference. All suggested cooking times in the adjacent general guidelines and the recipes that follow are for patties that are between ¾ and 1 inch thick and are at room temperature when they are placed over fairly hot, direct heat.

Cooking

Three cooking methods produce successful burgers. Grilling imparts a wonderful smoky flavor; broiling is quick and easy; and pancooking assures juicy patties and is my first choice when I don't want to fire up a grill.

GRILLING. Burgers may be grilled by direct heat or indirect heat. With direct-heat grilling, the patties are placed right over the heat source so they cook quickly, well charred on the outside and moist and juicy inside. They must be watched carefully to avoid burning or overcooking. Indirect-heat grilling offsets the patties from the fire, a practice highly recommended for burgers with high fat content or dripping marinades.

Preparing a fire in an electric or gas grill is as easy as throwing a switch or turning on a jet and striking a match. An electric grill is ready for cooking in three to four minutes; a gas fire is preheated in only a couple of minutes longer. With each unit, follow directions in the manufacturer's manual for preheating for direct-heat or indirect-heat grilling.

When preparing a fire in a charcoal grill, mound the briquettes or chunks of natural pure-carbon lump charcoal on the fuel grate and use your favorite method of starting a fire. I prefer an electric starter or a metal chimney. Allow 20 to 30 minutes for the fire to reach the proper stage for cooking burgers.

To prepare a charcoal fire for direct-heat grilling, allow the coal mound to burn undisturbed until lightly covered with white ash and glowing but no longer flaming. Using long-handled tongs, distribute the coals in an even layer over the fuel grate. If you wish to create areas with varying degrees of heat in order to move food around and to help prevent flare-ups, leave a few coals banked together and spread the others out evenly, allotting a little space with no coals.

To prepare a charcoal fire for indirect-heat grilling in a covered grill, allow the coals to reach the glowing ash stage, then position them along opposite sides of the fuel grate. In most cases you'll want to add a heavy-duty foil pan in between the rows of coals to catch burger drips that can cause flare-ups.

When the fire is ready, lightly brush the hot grill rack with vegetable oil. Add the patties and cook, turning once, until done to each diner's preference, about four minutes per side for medium-rare beef or lamb. If the patties are cooking too fast on the outside, move them to a cooler section of the grill. Some cooks like to turn the patties several times during grilling to ensure even cooking. If adding cheese, wait until you have turned the patties and they are within a few minutes of being done, then top with sliced, shredded, or crumbled cheese. Close the lid for quicker melting.

BROILING. Insert a grill rack into a metal broiler pan, position the pan so that the meat will be about four inches from the heat source, and preheat the broiler to hot. Lightly brush the hot grill rack with vegetable oil, place the patties on the rack, and slip the pan under the broiler. Cook the patties about four minutes on one side, then turn and broil until done to each diner's preference, about four minutes longer for medium-rare beef or lamb.

If the meat is very lean, you may brush it with a bit of melted butter, olive oil, or high-quality vegetable oil before and during broiling.

PANCOOKING. Also known as panfrying or flat-grilling, this quick-and-easy method produces juicy patties. If the meat has an average amount of fat and the fat is fairly evenly distributed, burgers may be cooked in an ungreased heavy skillet. If the meat is very lean, such as ground sirloin or veal, you will need to add enough fat to the pan to form a thin film over the bottom before adding the patties. In lieu of oil or butter, you may use a small piece of trimmed meat fat and heat it until it melts and coats the bottom of the pan with a film of rendered fat; discard the piece of fat.

If using very lean meat, heat about one tablespoon oil or unsalted butter or a small piece of trimmed beef fat in a heavy sauté pan, skillet, or griddle over high heat. If the meat contains some fat, omit the fat, place the dry pan over high heat, and sprinkle a fine layer of salt over the bottom. When the cooking fat is very hot but not quite brown or when the salt in a dry pan begins to brown and the pan is almost but not quite smoking, add the patties; the meat should begin sizzling the moment it touches the hot metal. Cook until well browned on the bottom, two to three minutes. Using a wide spatula, turn the patties. Reduce the heat to medium-low and cook, turning several times to ensure even cooking, until the burger is done to each diner's preference, about 8 minutes' total cooking time for medium-rare beef or lamb.

SERVING

Burgers taste best when the buns or other breads are warm and lightly toasted.

Even when toasted, buns slathered with spreads or sauces get soggy in a hurry. I prefer to let diners add their own condiments when the burgers are served.

In addition to the usual side dish of fries or chips, consider coleslaw, potato salad, cold pastas, rice salads, marinated vegetables, green salads, baked beans, corn-on-the-cob, or grilled vegetables to round out the meal.

Burgers are equally at home with a glass of wine, a cold beer, iced tea, your favorite soda, a milk shake, or a malt.

FAVORITE STANDARDS

Here are my secrets for great burgers. Following my basic recipe are numerous variations that offer international flavors, and then comes a handful of more unusual preparations. Be sure to check the index in my *Beef Cookbook* for other burger recipes.

Basic Beef Burgers

Most burger cooks agree that chuck or beef with a little fat cooks up particularly juicy and flavorful. Chopped sirloin, round, or other tender lean beef renders a less fatty burger, but will probably need brushing with a little oil or melted butter during cooking to prevent sticking.

In a bowl, combine the beef with salt and pepper to taste; be generous with the pepper. Handling the beef as little as possible to avoid compacting it, mix well. Divide the meat into 4 equal portions and form the portions into patties to fit the bread.

To grill the burgers, prepare a hot fire for direct-heat cooking in a grill. When the fire is ready, brush the grill rack with vegetable oil. Place the patties on the grill and cook until browned on the bottom, about 4 minutes. Using a wide spatula, turn the patties. Sprinkle each patty with Worcestershire sauce to taste and then top with a small dollop of butter. Cook until done to preference, about 4 minutes longer for medium-rare. During the last few minutes of cooking, lightly brush the cut side of the bread with olive oil or butter and place the bread, cut side down, on the outer edges of the grill to toast lightly and top each patty with cheese to melt.

To pancook the burgers, place a heavy skillet or griddle over high heat and sprinkle a fine layer of salt over the bottom. When the salt begins to brown and the pan is almost but not quite smoking, add the patties and cook until well browned on the bottom, about 3 minutes. Using a wide spatula, turn the patties, reduce the heat to medium-low, and cook, turning several times, until done to preference, about 5 minutes longer for medium-rare beef or lamb. A few minutes before the burger is ready, top each patty with a slice of the cheese. Meanwhile, lightly toast the buns in a toaster or under a preheated broiler. Lightly brush the toasted bread with olive oil or butter.

Transfer the patties to the bottom halves of the bread sections or buns. Cover with the bread or bun tops. Offer condiments at the table.

Serves 4.

1½ pounds ground beef (see recipe introduction)
Salt
Freshly ground black pepper
Loaf of French bread, cut into 4 sections each 5 to 6 inches long and then split lengthwise, or 4 Whole-Wheat Hamburger Buns (page 86) or other hamburger buns, split
Vegetable oil for brushing on grill rack (if grilling)
About ¼ cup Worcestershire sauce
About 4 teaspoons unsalted butter
Sliced or crumbled good-melting cheese (see sidebar on page 14 for suggested cheeses)
Olive oil or melted unsalted butter for brushing on buns

CONDIMENTS
Grilled red or yellow onion slices, or raw red onion slices
Mayonnaise (page 91), made with garlic if desired, or high-quality commercial mayonnaise
Mustard of choice
Vine-ripened tomato slices
Fresh basil leaves, tender lettuce leaves, or other young greens

CHEESEBURGERS

I can't remember the name of the old Hollywood film or of the actress in it (sounds like a Tallulah Bankhead role) who played the poor grand lady who snootily queried, "And what, may I ask, is a cheeseburger?" Thank heavens most of us are more burger literate.

Any burger can be turned into a cheeseburger by topping it with a slice of cheese or a mound of freshly shredded or crumbled cheese after the final turning. Allow two to three minutes for most cheeses to melt; actual time depends on heat source and type of cheese.

Some cooks like to encase the cheese inside the patty, where it melts for a creamy surprise when you bite into the burger. Although I occasionally use this method, I find that it can be a bit tricky. If the cheese is too cold, for instance, it may not melt by the time the meat is done to rare or medium-rare, or the cheese may become just a runny mess that makes the burger difficult to eat.

My favorite cheeses for burgers include Italian Fontina and Gorgonzola, any creamy blue, Swiss Gruyère or Emmenthaler, Canadian white Cheddar, and California jalapeño jack or creamy goat's milk cheese.

INTERNATIONAL VARIATIONS

Although the burger is indisputedly American, it can be given a variety of accents that evoke a cook's tour of the world. The amounts given below are for one pound of meat. Adjust seasonings to taste.

Asian Burgers. Combine equal parts ground pork and beef. Season the meats with 1 tablespoon minced fresh ginger root, 1 tablespoon minced or pressed garlic, 3 tablespoons soy sauce, and a few drops hot chile oil. Top with stir-fried bean sprouts and sprigs of fresh cilantro (coriander).

Caribbean Burgers. Add about 3 tablespoons dried jerk seasoning to the meat. Top the cooked patties with freshly made citrus salsa.

French Burgers. Season ground veal with salt and pepper to taste and form into patties. Melt ¼ cup (½ stick) unsalted butter in a small saucepan. Add 2 tablespoons minced shallot and 1 cup minced fresh mushrooms, preferably chanterelle or other wild varieties, and sauté until soft, about 3 minutes. Stir in ¾ cup dry red wine; ¼ cup minced fresh chervil, parsley, or other herb; and 1 tablespoon Worcestershire sauce. Cook over high heat until the sauce is reduced by half. Pancook the burgers, place on toasted French bread slices, and pour the sauce over the top.

German Burgers. Season ground beef with salt and pepper to taste and form into patties. Pull bacon strips to stretch slightly and cut if necessary to adjust length to wrap around the circumference of the patties, overlapping slightly at the end. Wrap a bacon strip around each patty to form a collar and secure with a wooden pick. Grill or broil until meat is done to your preference and the bacon is crisp. Serve on toasted buns or onion rolls with German mustard and lots of grilled onion.

Italian Burgers. Combine equal parts hot or mild crumbled Italian sausage and ground beef. Melt Fontina cheese on top, if desired. Top with grilled or sautéed red sweet peppers and onions.

Korean Burgers. In a bowl, combine 1 cup soy sauce, ½ cup sugar, ¼ cup Asian-style sesame oil, 2 teaspoons minced or pressed garlic, ½ cup finely chopped green onion, and 1 teaspoon freshly ground black pepper. Prepare small beef patties, place in the bowl with the marinade, and let stand for 2 hours at room temperature. Grill the patties, brushing with some of the marinade during cooking. Serve the patties with chilled crisp lettuce leaves for wrapping and eating out of hand. For condiments, offer kimchee (pickled cabbage, available in Asian groceries and some supermarkets), shredded daikon (white radish), minced fresh hot chiles, fresh bean sprouts, minced green onion, toasted sesame seeds, and hot chile sauce or hot bean paste.

Mexican Burgers. Add 3 tablespoons ground dried chile, 1 tablespoon dried cumin, and 2 tablespoons minced fresh chiles to the beef. Top with jalapeño jack cheese, if desired. Mound shredded crisp lettuce on cooked patties. Offer mayonnaise flavored with minced canned *chipolte* chiles (smoked jalapeños) packed in *adobo* sauce.

Middle Eastern Burgers. Soak 2 slices whole-wheat bread in warm water to cover until soft. Squeeze bread to press out excess moisture and then break them into pieces. Mix the bread with 1 pound ground lamb, ¼ cup plain yogurt, 1 tablespoon minced or pressed garlic, ½ cup minced fresh cilantro (coriander) or mint, 2 teaspoons curry powder, 1½ teaspoons ground cumin, ½ teaspoon ground cardamom, ¼ teaspoon ground turmeric, and salt and ground cayenne pepper to taste. Form into patties and grill. Serve on heated pita bread with plain yogurt flavored to taste with grated onion and cucumber, minced fresh mint, and ground cayenne pepper.

Pacific Island Burgers. Season ground beef or chicken with salt and pepper to taste and form into patties. Brush with teriyaki sauce before and during cooking. Top with grilled or broiled pineapple slices or fruit chutney.

AMERICAN CLASSICS

BACON CHEESEBURGERS. Melt Cheddar cheese on the patties and crown each with 2 slices crisply cooked bacon. Serve on sesame seed buns with red onion rings, tender lettuce leaves, sliced ripe tomato, and bread-and-butter pickles. Offer yellow mustard, mayonnaise, and catsup. Or upscale this perennial favorite with Italian Fontina topped with cooked *pancetta*.

MUSHROOM BURGERS. Sauté sliced fresh mushrooms in butter and spoon over cooked patties. Sensational when prepared with such flavorful varieties as chanterelles, porcini, or shiitakes.

NEW YORK BURGERS. Keep it simple. Just good beef on a bun with sliced onion and offer Dijon-style mustard and catsup.

ONION BURGERS. Although many people add onion soup mix or onion powder to raw beef, I opt for seasoning 1 pound beef with ½ cup minced or grated yellow onion and about 2 teaspoons minced or pressed garlic along with the salt and pepper. For a double whammy, crown the cooked patties with caramelized or grilled onion.

Catahoula Parish Venison Burgers with Pear Relish

Mother's Pear Relish (page 90)
1 pound venison
3 to 4 ounces pork fat or beef fat
Salt
Freshly ground black pepper
4 hamburger buns, split
Worcestershire sauce or steak sauce
Vegetable oil for brushing on grill
    rack
Red or yellow onion slices

My father, a longtime resident of Catahoula Parish, Louisiana, is an avid deer hunter. Although I never felt comfortable joining in on the kill, I always enjoyed the bounty. For as long as I can remember, my parents have made these burgers.

Since venison, whether from deer, elk, or moose, contains little fat, my folks always add a bit of beef or pork fat when grinding the venison. Mother says that although pork fat renders a better burger, she now uses beef fat because the patties keep longer in the freezer. She freezes a mountain of patties during hunting season for year-round enjoyment.

In lieu of my mother's relish, which she cans in quantity during pear season, offer your own favorite condiments.

About 1 week before cooking the burgers, prepare the relish and store in a cool place.

In a meat grinder or food processor, grind the venison and pork fat or beef fat together.

In a bowl, combine the ground meat with salt and pepper to taste. Handling the meat as little as possible to avoid compacting it, mix well. Divide the mixture into 4 equal portions and form the portions into patties to fit the buns. Place the patties on a platter and sprinkle to taste with Worcestershire sauce or steak sauce. Cover and let stand at room temperature for about 30 minutes.

In a grill with a cover, prepare a medium-hot fire for direct-heat cooking.

When the fire is ready, brush the grill rack with vegetable oil. Place the patties on the grill and cook until browned on the bottom, about 4 minutes. With a wide spatula, turn the patties and cook until done to preference, about 4 minutes longer for medium-rare. During the last few minutes of cooking, place the buns, cut side down, on the outer edges of the grill to toast lightly.

Spread the relish on the cut sides of the toasted buns. On the bottom half of each bun, place a burger. Top with an onion slice and then with the bun top.

Serves 4.

Chili Burgers

While I love the taste of chili with a burger, I despise the idea of chili ladled over a patty so that it has to be eaten with a fork. In this version, the chili flavor is there, but you can pick it up and eat it like a real burger. I serve these zesty burgers between hand-made thick tortillas or wrap them inside large, regular corn tortillas The patties are also good with cheese-flavored buns or sandwich rolls. To make your own, add grated Cheddar cheese to a basic bread dough.

In a small bowl, combine the sour cream and mayonnaise and stir until smooth. Set aside.

In a sauté pan or skillet, heat the vegetable oil over medium-high heat. Add the onion and sauté until soft, about 5 minutes. Add the garlic, ground chile, and cumin and sauté for 1 minute longer. Remove from the heat and set aside.

In a grill, prepare a hot fire for direct-heat cooking.

In a large bowl, combine the beef with salt and pepper to taste. Add the sautéed onion mixture, tomato paste, and minced cilantro. Handling the beef as little as possible to avoid compacting it, mix well. Divide the meat into 4 equal portions and form the portions into patties to fit the buns, or shape into rectangles to fit over one half of a tortilla.

When the fire is ready, brush the grill rack with vegetable oil. Place the patties on the grill and cook until browned on the bottom, about 4 minutes. With a wide spatula, turn the patties and cook until done to preference, about 4 minutes longer for medium-rare.

Meanwhile, if using thick tortillas, pour enough oil in a heavy skillet to form a thin film on the bottom of the pan. Preheat the oil and pancook the tortillas until lightly browned but not crisp. If using thin tortillas, wrap them in foil and place them on the grill to heat. If using buns, lightly brush the cut sides with oil or butter and place them, cut side down, on the outer edges of the grill to toast lightly during the last few minutes of cooking the burgers.

On 4 of the thick tortillas or the bottom half of each bun, place a patty and cover with another tortilla or a bun top. Or enclose each patty in a large, thin tortilla. Offer the mayonnaise mixture and condiments at the table.

Serves 4.

¼ cup sour cream
¼ cup Mayonnaise (page 91) or high-quality commercial mayonnaise
2 tablespoons canola oil or other high-quality vegetable oil
1 cup finely chopped yellow onion
2 teaspoons minced or pressed garlic
3 tablespoons ground dried hot chiles such as *ancho* or *pasilla*, or to taste
1½ teaspoons ground cumin, or to taste
1½ pounds ground beef, preferably chuck
Salt
Freshly ground black pepper
3 tablespoons tomato paste
3 tablespoons minced fresh cilantro (coriander)
4 thick corn tortillas; 4 large, thin corn tortillas; or 4 hamburger buns, preferably cheese-flavored, split
Vegetable oil for brushing on grill rack and cooking tortillas
Olive oil or melted unsalted butter for brushing on buns

CONDIMENTS
Freshly grated Cheddar cheese
Chopped red onion
Fresh cilantro sprigs
Sliced pickled jalapeño chiles or other hot chiles
Salsa

Knecht Burgers

1½ pounds ground lean beef
¼ cup finely chopped yellow onion
2 tablespoons Worcestershire sauce, or to taste
Salt
1 sweet French or Italian baguette, about 2½ inches wide, split lengthwise, or 4 small French rolls, split
Unsalted butter, softened, for spreading
Dijon-style or yellow American mustard

The first time I was served these little baked burgers was at a Christmas party hosted by Dorothy Knecht (pronounced "connect"), the vivacious aunt of my late partner Lin Cotton. I couldn't stop eating them. Baked in a blistering hot oven, the French bread gets crisp and the juice from the lean beef permeates the bread.

Dorothy makes these burgers by the score and freezes them for a quick-and-easy party appetizer or unexpected lunch guests. For a large group, she opts for onion powder in place of the chopped onion, spreads the meat mixture on split baguettes, and cooks them before slicing crosswise into individual portions. For smaller groups, she purchases small French rolls and makes individual burgers. In any case, be sure that the meat covers all exposed top surfaces of the bread to prevent the bread from burning around the edges during the high-heat cooking. The burgers may also be served in larger portions as a main course.

Add minced fresh herbs, chopped mushrooms, or other seasonings to the beef for variety. Dorothy also likes to add a touch of MSG.

In a bowl, combine the beef, onion, Worcestershire sauce, and salt to taste.

Preheat an oven to 400° F.

Spread the bread with a thin coating of the butter. Spread the meat mixture over the bread in an even layer about ¼ inch thick. Be sure that the meat covers the edges of the bread; any exposed bread will burn. Press the meat down around the edges with a fork or your fingers to adhere it to the bread. Spread a layer of mustard to taste over the meat. Place the bread on ungreased baking sheets.

Transfer the burgers to the hot oven and cook until done to preference, about 6 to 7 minutes for medium-rare.

If using a baguette, transfer the halves to a cutting surface and cut each piece crosswise into 8 equal sections, or as desired.

Serves 8 as a starter, or 4 as a main dish.

New California Patty Melts

3 tablespoons unsalted butter
2 cups thinly sliced yellow onion
1 pound ground beef
2 teaspoons Worcestershire sauce, or
    to taste
Salt
Freshly ground black pepper
8 rye bread slices
4 ounces creamy goat's milk cheese
Vegetable oil for brushing on grill
    rack
Variety of mustards

Chèvre and caramelized onion add an updated taste to this Los Angeles classic usually made with Cheddar and grilled onion.

In a sauté pan or skillet, melt the butter over medium heat. Add the onion, cover, reduce the heat to low, and cook for 15 minutes. Remove the cover and cook the onion until very soft and golden, about 45 minutes longer. Remove from the heat and keep warm.

In a grill, prepare a hot fire for direct-heat cooking, or preheat a broiler.

In a bowl, combine the beef, Worcestershire sauce, and salt and pepper to taste. Handling the meat as little as possible to avoid compacting it, mix well. Divide the beef into 8 equal portions and form the portions into thin, round patties to fit the bread slices. Cut the cheese into 4 pieces a little smaller than the patties. Place a piece of cheese on 4 of the patties, cover with the remaining patties, and press the edges together to seal and encase the cheese.

When the fire is ready, brush the grill rack or broiler rack with vegetable oil. Place the patties on the grill rack or under the broiler and cook until browned on the bottom, about 4 minutes. With a wide spatula, turn the patties and cook until done to preference, about 4 minutes longer for medium-rare. During the last few minutes of cooking, place the bread slices on the outer edges of the grill to toast lightly or prepare in a toaster.

Top 4 slices of the bread with the patties, pile on the onion, and cover with the remaining bread slices. Offer mustards at the table.

Serves 4.

Barbecued Chicken Burgers

About 2 cups barbecue sauce (see recipe introduction)
2 pounds ground chicken meat
Salt
Freshly ground black pepper
6 hamburger buns, split
Vegetable oil for brushing on grill rack
6 slices smoked Gouda cheese (optional)

CONDIMENTS
Thin red onion slices, separated into rings
Kosher dill pickle slices
Fresh cilantro (coriander) sprigs

Use a favorite recipe to make barbecue sauce, purchase a high-quality commercial sauce, or see page 84 in my *Chicken* cookbook. If you choose ground chicken breast, you may need to add a lightly beaten egg to help bind the low-fat meat together during cooking.

Prepare the sauce. Set aside.

In a grill, prepare a medium-hot fire for direct-heat cooking.

In a large bowl, combine the chicken and a little salt and pepper. Handling the meat as little as possible to avoid compacting it, mix well. Divide the mixture into 6 equal portions and form the portions into round patties to fit the buns.

When the fire is ready, brush the grill rack with vegetable oil. Place the patties on the grill rack, brush the tops with barbecue sauce, and cook until browned on the bottom, about 4 minutes. With a wide spatula, turn the patties and cook, brushing frequently with the sauce, until the juices run clean when the patties are pierced, about 4 minutes longer. During the last few minutes of cooking, place the buns, cut side down, on the outer edges of the grill to toast lightly and top each patty with a cheese slice (if used) to melt.

Transfer the patties to the bottom halves of the buns and cover with the bun tops. Offer the condiments, including additional barbecue sauce, at the table.

Serves 6.

Cranberry-Glazed Turkey Burgers

This low-fat burger has all the flavors of an autumn feast. If you can afford the calories and fat, a couple of crisp bacon strips on each burger adds delectable crunch.

In a grill, prepare a medium-hot fire for direct-heat cooking.

In a large bowl, combine the turkey, minced or crumbled sage and thyme, orange zest, and a little salt and pepper. Handling the meat as little as possible to avoid compacting it, mix well. Divide the mixture into 6 equal portions and form the portions into round patties to fit the buns.

When the fire is ready, brush the grill rack with vegetable oil. Place the patties on the grill rack, brush the tops with the melted cranberry sauce, and cook until browned on the bottom, about 4 minutes. With a large spatula, carefully turn the patties and cook, brushing frequently with the sauce, until the patty tests opaque when cut into with a small, sharp knife, about 4 minutes longer. During the last few minutes of cooking, place the buns, cut side down, on the outer edges of the grill to toast lightly.

Transfer the patties to the bottom halves of the buns and cover with the bun tops. Garnish plates with the sage leaves. Offer the condiments at the table.

Serves 6.

2 pounds ground turkey
6 tablespoons minced fresh sage, or
    2 tablespoons crumbled dried sage
3 tablespoons minced fresh thyme, or
    1 tablespoon crumbled dried
    thyme
3 tablespoons grated or minced
    orange zest
Salt
Freshly ground black pepper
Whole-Wheat Hamburger Buns
    (page 86), split, or 6 other
    hamburger buns, split
Vegetable oil for brushing on grill
    rack
Jellied cranberry sauce, melted for
    brushing on patties
Fresh sage leaves for garnish

CONDIMENTS
Whole berry cranberry sauce or
    relish, preferably freshly made
Mayonnaise (page 91) or high-quality
    commercial mayonnaise
Tender, young spinach leaves

Nut Burgers

The recipe for these rich vegetarian burgers comes from my Lake Tahoe friends Meri McEneny and Jan Ellis. Although the nuts and seeds may be used raw, toasting them in a pan on the stove top or in an oven before grinding adds to the flavor. Meri and Jan often toss the nuts and seeds in soy sauce before toasting.

These patties are very fragile and tend to fall apart. Use two wide spatulas to turn the burgers on a grill and push them back together if they split, or place them in a hinged grill basket for easier turning.

Prepare the mayonnaise. Cover and refrigerate.

In a nut grinder or a food processor, finely grind the cashews or almonds, pecans or walnuts, and sunflower seeds.

In a large bowl, combine the ground nuts and seeds, carrot, onion, celery, garlic, flour, egg or lecithin, and soy sauce and pepper to taste. If the mixture seems too dry to hold together, blend in just enough water to moisten. Mix well. Divide the mixture into 4 or 5 equal portions and form the portions into round patties to fit the buns. Cover and chill for about 1 hour.

In a grill, prepare a medium-hot fire for direct-heat cooking. Or preheat a heavy skillet for pancooking.

When the fire or pan is ready, brush the grill rack or pan with vegetable oil. Place the patties on the rack or in the pan and cook until browned on the bottom, about 4 minutes. Using a wide spatula, very carefully turn the patties and cook until well browned, firm to the touch, and no longer gooey when cut into with a small, sharp knife, about 5 minutes longer. During the last few minutes of cooking, place the buns, cut side down, on the outer edges of the grill or, cut side up, under a preheated broiler to toast lightly.

Transfer the patties to the bottom halves of the buns and cover with the bun tops. Offer the condiments, including the mayonnaise, at the table.

Serves 4 or 5.

Sesame Mayonnaise (page 91)
1 cup cashews or almonds
1 cup pecans or walnuts
1 cup sunflower seeds
⅓ cup finely chopped carrot
⅓ cup finely chopped red onion
⅓ cup finely chopped celery
1 teaspoon minced or pressed garlic, or to taste
2 tablespoons whole-wheat flour or all-purpose flour
1 egg, lightly beaten, or 1 tablespoon liquid lecithin (available in natural-foods stores) to bind ingredients
About 1 tablespoon soy sauce, preferably tamari
Freshly ground black pepper
1 to 2 tablespoons water (optional)
4 or 5 Whole-Wheat Hamburger Buns (page 86), split, or other hamburger buns, split
Vegetable oil for brushing on grill rack

CONDIMENTS
Assorted tender greens
Thin red onion slices, separated into rings

AWARD WINNERS

Sutter Home Winery has graciously consented to share recipes from its Build A Better Burger national cookoff. Contestants are required to use a Weber kettle grill, thus each recipe in this section calls for a grill with a cover. The burgers may also be cooked successfully on an uncovered grill, under a broiler, or in a stove-top pan.

Napa Valley Basil-Smoked Burgers

⅔ cup light mayonnaise
2 tablespoons basil pesto (use a
  favorite recipe)
2 pounds ground sirloin
¼ cup Sutter Home Zinfandel
¼ cup lightly packed minced fresh
  basil
¼ cup minced red onion
¼ cup fine fresh Italian bread crumbs
8 sun-dried tomatoes packed in oil,
  drained and finely chopped
1 to 2 teaspoons garlic salt
6 large seeded sandwich rolls, split
Vegetable oil for brushing on grill
  rack
8 fresh basil sprigs, moistened with
  water for tossing onto the fire
6 slices Monterey jack cheese
Red leaf lettuce leaves
6 large tomato slices, about ¼ inch
  thick
Paper-thin red onion slices, separated
  into rings
Fresh basil sprigs (optional)

Jim Pleasants of Williamsburg, Virginia, walked away with the Grand Prize of $10,000 at the first Build A Better Burger national cookoff. I've included Mr. Pleasants's directions for adding fresh basil sprigs to the fire, although I don't find that they add anything to the sensational combination of flavors in these burgers.

For the photo, I've served fried beet chips alongside the burger.

In a grill with a cover, prepare a medium-hot fire for direct-heat cooking.

In a small bowl, combine the mayonnaise and pesto; set aside.

In a bowl, combine the sirloin, Zinfandel, minced basil, minced onion, bread crumbs, sun-dried tomatoes, and garlic salt to taste. Handling the meat as little as possible to avoid compacting it, mix well. Divide the meat mixture into 6 equal portions and form the portions into round patties to fit the rolls.

When the fire is ready, brush the grill rack with vegetable oil. Toss the moistened basil sprigs directly onto the coals, then place the patties on the grill, cover, and cook until browned on the bottom, about 4 minutes. With a wide spatula, turn the patties and cook until done to preference, about 4 minutes longer for medium-rare. During the last few minutes of cooking, place the rolls, cut side down, on the outer edges of the grill to toast lightly and top each patty with a cheese slice to melt.

Spread the mayonnaise on the toasted rolls. On the bottom half of each roll, layer the lettuce, burger, tomato slice, and onion ring. Add basil sprigs, if desired, and cover with the roll tops.

Serves 6.

Lamburgers à la Grecque with Cilantro-Mint Chutney

On a gorgeous late-summer afternoon in the Napa Valley, Robert Chirico of Greenfield, Massachusetts, grilled his way to a $10,000 Grand Prize with this recipe.

To make the chutney, combine all the ingredients in a blender or food processor and blend thoroughly. Cover and chill for at least several hours or as long as 24 hours.

In a grill with a cover, prepare a medium-hot fire, preferably with natural hardwood charcoal, for direct-heat cooking.

To make the burgers, combine the sirloin, lamb, garlic, cheese, olives, and salt in a large bowl. Handling the meat as little as possible to avoid compacting it, mix well. Divide the mixture into 6 equal portions and form the portions into round patties to fit the pita breads. Brush the patties with the olive oil and then sprinkle with the cumin mixture.

When the fire is ready, brush the grill rack with vegetable oil. Place the patties on the grill, cover, and cook until browned on the bottom, about 4 minutes. With a wide spatula, turn the patties and cook until done to preference, about 4 minutes longer for medium-rare. During the last few minutes of cooking, place the pita breads on the outer edges of the grill and turn to toast lightly on both sides.

Place the patties inside the pita bread pockets and add the chutney. Offer the condiments at the table.

Serves 6.

CILANTRO-MINT CHUTNEY
⅓ cup plain yogurt
2 tablespoons chopped yellow onion
1½ fresh jalapeño chiles, stemmed, seeded, and chopped
1½ tablespoons chopped fresh ginger root
¾ cup fresh cilantro (coriander) leaves
⅓ cup fresh mint leaves
1 large garlic clove, chopped
½ teaspoon salt, preferably kosher
Pinch of sugar

LAMBURGERS
1 pound lean ground sirloin
1 pound lean ground lamb
1 garlic clove, minced
½ cup crumbled feta cheese (about 2 ounces)
⅓ cup minced pitted Kalamata olives
1 teaspoon salt, preferably kosher
6 medium-sized pita breads, preferably thicker variety
¼ cup fruity olive oil, preferably extra-virgin
1 teaspoon ground cumin mixed with 1 teaspoon ground coriander
Vegetable oil for brushing on grill rack

CONDIMENTS
Tomato slices
Thin red onion slices
Red leaf lettuce leaves

Mustard-Grilled Lamb Burgers with Eggplant Salsa

BASIL YOGURT
½ cup low-fat plain yogurt
2 tablespoons chopped fresh basil
½ cup sour cream

GRILLED EGGPLANT SALSA
1 large eggplant, sliced crosswise
    ¾ inch thick
¼ cup olive oil, preferably
    extra-virgin
½ teaspoon chile powder
1 teaspoon salt
1 teaspoon ground cumin
Vegetable oil for brushing on grill
    rack
½ small yellow onion, unpeeled
2 tablespoons diced, canned roasted
    red sweet pepper
1 tablespoon balsamic vinegar or red
    wine vinegar

BURGERS
1¼ pounds ground extra-lean lamb
1¼ cups minced fresh mushrooms
    (about 5 ounces)
½ cup (about 2½ ounces) chopped
    hazelnuts (filberts)
1 garlic clove, minced or pressed
1 egg white, lightly beaten
1 teaspoon salt
¼ teaspoon freshly ground black
    pepper
8 hamburger buns, split
Vegetable oil for brushing on grill
    rack
Mustard for spreading on patties

Lettuce leaves

Betty Shenberger of Beaverton, Oregon, ended up in second place at the first Build A Better Burger contest.

To make the Basil Yogurt, combine the yogurt and basil in a blender or a food processor and blend well. Remove to a bowl and fold in the sour cream. Cover and chill.

In a grill with a cover, prepare a medium-hot fire for direct-heat cooking.

To make the salsa, brush both sides of each eggplant slice with some of the olive oil. In a small bowl, stir together the chile powder, salt, and cumin. Sprinkle the spice mixture on both sides of each eggplant slice.

Brush the grill rack with vegetable oil. Place the eggplant slices on the grill, cover, and cook, turning once, until very brown on both sides, 5 to 7 minutes on each side. Meanwhile, brush the onion half with olive oil. Grill, covered, until the skin is crisp and blackened. Remove the eggplant and onion to a plate to cool. Slip off and discard the skins from the eggplant and onion, then chop coarsely. In a bowl, lightly combine the eggplant, onion, red pepper, and vinegar; set aside.

To make the burgers, combine the lamb, mushrooms, hazelnuts, garlic, egg white, salt, and pepper in a bowl. Handling the meat as little as possible to avoid compacting it, mix well. Divide the meat mixture into 8 equal portions and form the portions into round patties to fit the buns.

When the fire is ready, brush the grill rack with vegetable oil. Place the patties on the grill, cover, and cook until browned on the bottom, about 4 minutes. With a wide spatula, turn the patties, spread the tops of the patties with mustard, and cook until done to preference, about 4 minutes longer for medium-rare. During the last few minutes of cooking, place the buns, cut side down, on the outer edges of the grill to toast lightly.

Serve the burgers and toasted buns with the Eggplant Salsa, Basil Yogurt, and lettuce for guests to assemble as desired.

Serves 8.

Hazelnut-Crusted Lamb Burgers

2 pounds ground lamb
½ cup Sutter Home Cabernet
   Sauvignon
½ cup minced red onion
½ cup fine fresh Italian bread crumbs
2 tablespoons chopped fresh parsley
1 tablespoon chopped fresh basil, or
   1 teaspoon crumbled dried basil
1 tablespoon chopped fresh rosemary,
   or 1 teaspoon crumbled dried
   rosemary
1 tablespoon chopped fresh thyme, or
   1 teaspoon crumbled dried thyme
1 garlic clove, minced
½ teaspoon salt
¼ teaspoon freshly cracked black
   pepper
6 large sesame seed sandwich buns,
   split
½ cup chopped blanched hazelnuts
   (filberts)
¼ cup fine dry Italian bread crumbs
Vegetable oil for brushing on grill
   rack
6 tablespoons crumbled mild semisoft
   goat's milk cheese (about
   3 ounces)
Dijon-style mustard
Spinach leaves
6 large tomato slices

During her second trip to the Build A Better Burger national cookoff, Debbie Russell captured First Prize. She hails from Colorado Springs, Colorado.

In a grill with a cover, prepare a medium-hot fire for direct-heat cooking.

In a large bowl, combine the lamb, Cabernet Sauvignon, onion, fresh bread crumbs, parsley, basil, rosemary, thyme, garlic, salt, and pepper. Handling the meat as little as possible to avoid compacting it, mix well. Divide the mixture into 6 equal portions and form the portions into round patties to fit the buns.

On a plate, stir together the hazelnuts and dry bread crumbs. Press both sides of each patty into the nut mixture, coating evenly.

When the fire is ready, brush the grill rack with vegetable oil. Place the patties on the grill, cover, and cook until browned on the bottom, about 4 minutes. With a wide spatula, turn the patties and cook until done to preference, about 4 minutes longer for medium-rare. During the last few minutes of cooking, place the buns, cut side down, on the outer edges of the grill to toast lightly and top each patty with 1 tablespoon of the cheese to melt.

Spread about 1 teaspoon mustard on the cut side of each toasted bun half. On the bottom half of each bun, layer the spinach, patty, and tomato slice. Cover with the bun tops.

Serves 6.

Spicy Sausage Burgers with Roasted Pepper Relish

Californian Priscilla Yee of Concord ranked third in the Build A Better Burger cookoff with this creative recipe.

In a grill with a cover, prepare a medium-hot fire for direct-heat cooking.

To make the burgers, combine the turkey, andouille, onion, and thyme in a bowl. Handling the meat as little as possible to avoid compacting it, mix well. Divide the mixture into 4 equal portions and form the portions into oval patties to fit the rolls; set aside.

To make the relish, cut down the sides of the bell pepper, following the natural contours of the pepper and forming 4 large slices in all. Cut the chiles in half lengthwise; remove and discard the seeds.

When the fire is ready, brush the grill rack with vegetable oil. Brush the pepper slices and chile halves with olive oil, place them on the grill, cover, and cook, turning several times, until tender, 4 to 5 minutes on each side.

Meanwhile, pour the Zinfandel into a medium-sized saucepan and place on the grill rack alongside the peppers. Bring to a boil and cook until reduced to 1 tablespoon. Remove from the fire and stir in the onion, thyme, vinegar, sugar, 1 tablespoon olive oil, and mustard. When the peppers are tender, peel them and cut into julienne strips; add to the saucepan and mix well.

While the relish is cooking, place the patties on the grill, cover, and cook until the patties are browned on the bottom, about 4 minutes. With a wide spatula, turn the patties and cook until the juices run clear when the patties are pierced, 5 to 7 minutes longer. During the last few minutes of cooking, place the rolls, cut side down, on the outer edges of the grill rack to toast lightly.

Brush the cut sides of the toasted rolls with olive oil. Place a burger on the bottom half of each roll. Spoon some pepper relish over the burgers and add the roll tops.

Serves 4.

BURGER PATTIES
1 pound ground turkey
8 ounces andouille or other smoked spicy sausage, chopped
¼ cup finely chopped red onion
1 tablespoon chopped fresh thyme, or 1 teaspoon crumbled dried thyme
4 sourdough French rolls, split

ROASTED PEPPER RELISH
1 large red bell pepper
2 fresh Anaheim or *pasilla* chiles
Vegetable oil for brushing on grill rack
Olive oil for brushing on vegetables
¾ cup Sutter Home Zinfandel
½ cup chopped red onion
1 teaspoon minced fresh thyme, or ¼ teaspoon crumbled dried thyme
2 tablespoons cider vinegar
2 tablespoons firmly packed brown sugar
1 tablespoon olive oil
2 teaspoons Dijon-style mustard

Olive oil for brushing on French rolls

Italian Burgers with Confetti Salsa

Caryl Welsh of Clarksville, Maryland, won Second Prize in the second Build A Better Burger contest. She suggests the use of partially ripe mangoes if green ones are unavailable.

To make the salsa, combine all the ingredients in a bowl, adjusting amount of jalapeño to taste. Cover and set aside for about 1 hour, to allow flavors to blend.

In a grill with a cover, prepare a medium-hot fire for direct-heat cooking.

To make the burgers, in a large bowl, combine the sausage, turkey, olives, prunes, basil, parsley, and Zinfandel. Handling the meat as little as possible to avoid compacting it, mix well. Divide the mixture into 6 equal portions and form the portions into round patties to fit the buns.

When the fire is ready, brush the grill rack with vegetable oil. Place the patties on the grill, cover, and cook until browned on the bottom, about 4 minutes. With a wide spatula, turn the patties and cook until the juices run clear when the patties are pierced, 6 to 8 minutes longer. During the last few minutes of cooking, place the rolls, cut side down, on the outer edges of the grill to toast lightly.

Transfer the patties to the bottom halves of the toasted buns, add a spoonful of salsa to each burger, and cover with the bun tops.

Serves 6.

CONFETTI SALSA
1 large tomato, chopped
1 small green mango, peeled, pitted, and chopped
6 prunes, pitted and chopped
¼ cup chopped shallot
¼ cup chopped fresh cilantro (coriander)
1 garlic clove, minced or pressed
Juice of 1 lime
½ fresh jalapeño chile, diced, or to taste

ITALIAN BURGERS
1 pound hot Italian sausage, skinned and crumbled
1 pound ground turkey
⅔ cup small pimento-stuffed green olives, chopped
15 pitted prunes, chopped
½ teaspoon crumbled dried basil
1½ tablespoons chopped fresh parsley
¼ cup Sutter Home Zinfandel
6 seeded hamburger buns, split
Vegetable oil for brushing on grill rack

Calypso Burgers

1 pound ground turkey
½ pound bulk hot pork sausage
1 teaspoon salt
¼ teaspoon freshly ground black
   pepper
½ teaspoon ground cloves
¾ teaspoon curry powder
1 tablespoon freshly squeezed lime
   juice
6 seeded sandwich rolls, split
1 tablespoon olive oil
1 yellow onion, finely chopped
2 garlic cloves, minced
1 small red sweet pepper or ½ large
   red sweet pepper, stemmed,
   seeded, deribbed, and finely
   chopped
2 fresh jalapeño chiles, stemmed and
   minced
2 tablespoons molasses
¼ cup dark rum
1 teaspoon grated lime zest
1 small ripe tomato, seeded and diced,
   or ½ large ripe tomato, seeded
   and diced
1 tablespoon Angostura bitters,
   or to taste
Vegetable oil for brushing on grill
   rack

This spicy burger came from Dr. Helen Conwell of Fairhope, Alabama, who garnered a Third Prize in the Build A Better Burger cookoff.

In a grill with a cover, prepare a medium fire for direct-heat cooking.

In a bowl, combine the turkey, sausage, ½ teaspoon of the salt, black pepper, cloves, curry, and lime juice. Handling the meat as little as possible to avoid compacting it, mix well. Divide the mixture into 6 equal portions and form the portions into round patties to fit the rolls; set aside.

When the fire is ready, heat the olive oil in a medium-sized saucepan set on the grill. Add the onion, garlic, sweet pepper, and jalapeño and sauté until softened, about 5 minutes. Add the remaining ½ teaspoon salt, molasses, rum, and lime zest. Cook, stirring, until the liquid has nearly evaporated. Stir in the tomato and bitters and move the saucepan to the edge of the grill to keep warm.

Brush the grill rack with vegetable oil. Place the patties on the grill, cover, and cook until browned on the bottom, about 4 minutes. With a wide spatula, turn the patties and cook until the juices run clear when the patties are pierced, about 5 minutes longer. During the last few minutes of cooking, place the rolls, cut side down, on the outer edges of the grill to toast lightly.

Transfer the patties to the bottom halves of the rolls, spoon on some of the pepper-tomato mixture, and cover with the roll tops.

Serves 6.

Three-Nut Turkey Burgers with Tropical Fruit Salsa

Theodore Skiba from Tequesta, Florida, was awarded the Judge's Award for creativity for this zesty entry in the Build A Better Burger contest. If you can't find whole-wheat buns, use my recipe on page 86.

To make the salsa, cut half of the star fruit into ¼-inch dice. Slice the remaining star fruit crosswise and reserve for garnish. In a bowl, combine the diced star fruit, mango, grapes, banana, cantaloupe, pineapple, jalapeño, lime zest and juice, and orange juice. Stir well to blend, cover, and refrigerate for at least 1 hour or for up to 3 hours.

To make the burgers, coarsely chop 5 tablespoons of each type of nut. Heat the peanut oil in a nonstick skillet over medium-high heat. Add the chopped nuts and sauté until lightly toasted, about 5 minutes. Combine the toasted nuts with 1 cup of the cheese and set aside.

Grind the remaining 3 tablespoons of each of the nuts together in a nut grinder or food processor and set aside.

Divide the turkey into 8 equal portions and form into round patties to fit the buns. Distribute the nut mixture evenly over the tops of 4 of the patties. Cover with the remaining patties and press the edges together to seal. Spread the ground nuts on a flat plate and press both sides of each burger into the nuts, pressing for good adhesion.

In a grill with a cover, prepare a hot fire for direct-heat cooking.

When the fire is ready, brush the grill rack with vegetable oil. Place the patties on the grill, cover, and cook until browned on the bottom, about 4 minutes. With a wide spatula, turn the patties and cook until juices run clear when the patties are pierced, about 5 minutes longer. During the last few minutes of cooking, distribute the remaining 1 cup cheese evenly over the tops to melt and place the buns, cut side down, on the outer edges of the grill to toast lightly.

Spoon 2 to 3 tablespoons of the salsa on the bottom halves of the buns. Add the patties, top each with about 1 tablespoon salsa and a lettuce leaf, and cover with the bun tops.

Serves 4.

TROPICAL FRUIT SALSA
1 star fruit (carambola)
1 small ripe mango, peeled, pitted, and cut into ¼-inch dice
½ cup red seedless grapes, coarsely chopped
1 banana, peeled and cut into ½-inch dice
⅓ small cantaloupe, peeled, seeded, and cut into ¼-inch dice
½ cup diced (¼-inch) pineapple, fresh or canned in its own juice
1 fresh jalapeño chile, stemmed and cut into very small squares
Grated zest and juice of 1 lime
¼ cup freshly squeezed orange juice

3-NUT TURKEY BURGERS
½ cup (2 ounces) hazelnuts (filberts)
½ cup (2 ounces) almonds
½ cup (1½ ounces) walnuts
1 tablespoon peanut oil
2 cups shredded Monterey jack cheese (about 6 ounces)
1 pound lean ground turkey
4 whole-wheat hamburger buns, split
Vegetable oil for brushing on grill rack
Red leaf lettuce leaves

Foxy Loxburgers

1½ pounds fresh salmon, boned, skinned, and ground
1 teaspoon freshly squeezed lemon juice
1 tablespoon minced yellow onion
1 tablespoon minced fresh dill, or 1 teaspoon crumbled dried dill
1 tablespoon dry sherry
4 bagels, split
Vegetable oil for brushing on grill rack
3 ounces cream cheese, softened
1 tablespoon unsalted butter, melted
8 thin slices sweet onion such as Maui or Walla Walla
Fresh dill sprigs (optional)

This unique burger was prepared by Connie Emerson of Reno, Nevada, a finalist in the Build A Better Burger cookoff.

In a grill with a cover, prepare a medium-hot fire for direct-heat cooking.

In a bowl, combine the salmon, lemon juice, minced onion, minced dill, and sherry. Handling the salmon as little as possible to avoid compacting it, mix well. Divide the mixture into 8 equal portions and form into round patties to fit the bagels.

When the fire is ready, brush the grill rack with vegetable oil. Place the patties on the grill, cover, and cook until browned on the bottom, about 4 minutes. With a wide spatula, turn the patties and cook until the salmon just turns opaque when tested by cutting into with a small, sharp knife, 4 to 6 minutes longer. During the last few minutes of cooking, place the bagels, cut side down, on the outer edges of the grill to toast lightly.

Meanwhile, in a small bowl, combine the cream cheese and butter and blend thoroughly.

Spread the cream cheese mixture on the cut side of each warm bagel half, then top each half with an onion slice and a salmon patty. Top with dill sprigs, if desired.

Serves 8.

Hearty Southern Bean Burgers

Louisianian Wayne Fairchild of Shreveport originated this unique vegetarian burger that the judges thought deserved an award for creativity.

Although I've left the recipe as entered by Mr. Fairchild, I found the patties too soft to turn on the grill. They worked fine after adding three tablespoons all-purpose flour to the mixture instead of dusting with flour. In any case, handle the fragile patties carefully when turning them on the grill or they will break.

In a grill with a cover, prepare a medium fire for direct-heat cooking.

In a bowl, mash the peas with a fork. Add the onion, egg, salt, pepper, catsup, and Worcestershire sauce; mix well. Divide the mixture into 6 equal portions and form the portions into round patties to fit the buns. Lightly brush the patties on both sides with vegetable oil, then lightly dust with flour.

When the fire is ready, brush the grill rack with vegetable oil. Place the patties on the grill, cover, and cook until browned on the bottom, about 4 minutes. Using a wide spatula, very carefully turn the patties and cook until the patties are well browned, firm to the touch, and are no longer gooey when cut into with a small, sharp knife, 5 to 6 minutes longer. During the last few minutes of cooking, place the buns, cut side down, on the outer edges of the grill to toast lightly.

Serve the patties on the toasted buns and offer the condiments at the table.

Serves 6.

2 cups cooked black-eyed peas
1 yellow onion, chopped
1 egg, lightly beaten
¼ teaspoon salt
¼ teaspoon freshly ground black
    pepper
2 tablespoons tomato catsup
1 tablespoon Worcestershire sauce
6 hamburger buns, split
Vegetable oil for brushing on burgers
    and on grill rack
All-purpose flour for dusting

CONDIMENTS
Tomato slices
Lettuce leaves
Mustard of choice
Mayonnaise or sandwich spread
Catsup
Pickles

Mu Shu Burgers

8 ounces ground round
8 ounces ground veal
8 ounces ground pork
2 tablespoons light soy sauce
2 tablespoons dry sherry
2 tablespoons grated fresh ginger root
¼ cup finely chopped green onion, including some green tops
½ cup coarsely chopped bean sprouts
3 dried Chinese black mushrooms, soaked in warm water to cover for 30 minutes, drained, tough stems discarded, and coarsely chopped
1 teaspoon finely crushed toasted Sichuan peppercorns
Vegetable oil for brushing on grill rack
Hoisin sauce for brushing on pancakes
6 mu shu pancakes (also called Chinese or Mandarin pancakes or Peking doilies, available in Chinese markets), warmed
Coarsely chopped green onion, including some green tops

I found this recipe from Jacquelyn Paine of Baltimore to be among the most intriguing submissions to the Build A Better Burger cookoff.

In a grill with a cover, prepare a medium-hot fire for direct-heat cooking.

In a medium-sized bowl, combine the ground round, veal, and pork. In a small bowl, stir together the soy sauce, sherry, and ginger. Add the soy mixture, finely chopped green onion, bean sprouts, mushrooms, and Sichuan pepper to the meat mixture. Handling the meat as little as possible to avoid compacting it, mix well. Divide the mixture into 6 equal portions and form the portions into round or oval patties about ½ inch thick.

When the fire is ready, brush the grill rack with vegetable oil. Place the patties on the grill, cover, and cook until browned on the bottom, about 4 minutes. With a wide spatula, turn the patties and cook until done to preference, about 4 minutes on each side for medium-rare.

Spread 1 to 2 teaspoons hoisin sauce on each pancake. Place a burger on each pancake, sprinkle with the coarsely chopped green onion, then fold the pancakes over the patties.

Serves 6.

Oslo Burgers

Tacoma, Washington, resident Lois Dowling made it to the national burger cookoff with a burger that captures Scandinavian flavors.

In a grill with a cover, prepare a medium-hot fire for direct-heat cooking.

In a small bowl, stir together the sour cream, horseradish, cucumber, and nutmeg; set aside.

In a bowl, combine the beef, mushrooms, onion, bacon, and pepper. Handling the meat as little as possible to avoid compacting it, mix well. Divide the mixture into 3 equal portions and form the portions into patties to fit the bread slices.

When the fire is ready, brush the grill rack with vegetable oil. Place the patties on the grill, cover, and cook until browned on the bottom, about 4 minutes. With a wide spatula, turn the patties and cook until done to preference, about 4 minutes longer for medium-rare. During the last few minutes of cooking, place the bread slices, buttered side down, on the outer edges of the grill to toast lightly and place a cheese slice on each patty to melt.

Spread the sour cream mixture on the toasted side of each bread slice. Place the patties atop the sour cream-spread sides of 3 bread slices. Arrange 2 tomato slices, overlapping, on top of each patty. Top with the remaining bread slices, toasted sides down. Slice in half on the diagonal to serve.

Serves 3.

½ cup sour cream
1 teaspoon prepared horseradish
⅓ cup finely diced cucumber
¼ teaspoon freshly grated or ground nutmeg
1 pound ground beef
⅓ cup chopped fresh mushrooms
⅓ cup chopped green onion, including some green tops
⅓ cup crumbled crisply cooked bacon
½ teaspoon coarsely ground black pepper
6 pumpernickel bread slices, buttered on one side
Vegetable oil for brushing on grill rack
3 slices Jarlsberg cheese
6 large, thin tomato slices

CHEF SPECIALS

These days most creative upscale restaurants offer
burgers on their menu, so I asked a group of chefs
who I consider to be among
America's finest to share
their favorite burgers.

Matt Adams' Christy Hill Burgers

1 pound ground beef
Salt
Freshly ground black pepper
6 sourdough bread slices
Vegetable oil for brushing on cooking
    surface
6 slices crisply cooked bacon, or
    3 tablespoons finely chopped
    toasted hazelnuts (filberts) or
    macadamia nuts
3 slices Gorgonzola cheese
Thin red onion slices
Ripe beefsteak tomato slices
Mayonnaise (page 91) or high-quality
    commercial mayonnaise

Christy Hill in Tahoe City on the north shore of Lake Tahoe is one of my favorite restaurants. Although burgers do not appear on the menu, owner-chef Matt Adams regularly prepares them for his staff and family.

In addition to the more traditional recipe that follows, Matt suggests making patties from ground raw shrimp, seasoning them with salt and pepper, and then sautéing or broiling them until done. He then tops the shrimp burgers with a glaze of *salsa fresca* and thin slices of Monterey jalapeño cheese and melts the cheese under a preheated broiler before serving on grilled sourdough slices.

A final suggestion from this imaginative chef and his partner-wife Debbie is a sausage burger topped with melted Cheddar cheese and grilled onions, again served on sourdough bread.

In a bowl, combine the beef with salt and pepper to taste. Handling the meat as little as possible to avoid compacting it, mix well. Divide the beef into 3 equal portions and form the portions into patties to fit the bread slices.

In a grill, prepare a hot fire for direct-heat cooking. Alternatively, preheat a broiler, a heavy skillet, or a griddle until very hot. (If you are not using a broiler to cook the burgers, preheat one anyway, as it will be needed for melting the cheese.)

When heated, brush the grill rack, broiler rack, or inside of the skillet or griddle with vegetable oil. Add the patties and cook until browned on the bottom, about 4 minutes. With a wide spatula, turn the patties and cook until done to preference, about 5 minutes longer for medium-rare.

Place 2 bacon slices or 1 tablespoon of the nuts on each cooked patty, cover with a slice of the cheese, and place under a preheated broiler until the cheese melts, about 1 minute.

Meanwhile, grill or toast the bread slices. Place the patties on 3 of the bread slices and top with the onion and tomato slices. Spread the remaining bread slices with mayonnaise and cover the burgers.

Serves 3.

Craig Claiborne's Veal Burgers Cordon Bleu

New York Times food editor and cookbook author Craig Claiborne always serves this open-face "hamburger" on toast, preferably made from whole-wheat bread. He likes to toast the bread slices in a preheated 375° F oven for about eight minutes, then he turns and cooks the other side until crisp and golden.

Place the veal in a mixing bowl.

Grate the onion onto a square of cheesecloth. Gather the cheesecloth around the onion and squeeze to extract about 1 tablespoon of juice. Add the onion juice to the veal. Add the dill or parsley, bread crumbs, milk, nutmeg, and salt and pepper to taste. Handling the mixture as little as possible to avoid compacting it, mix well. Divide the veal into 8 equal portions and form the portions into thin patties to fit the bread slices.

Place 1 round of prosciutto on each of 4 patties. Cover with a slice of cheese, another round of prosciutto, and another circle of cheese; leave an uncovered border of meat around the prosciutto and cheese layers. Cover each layered patty neatly with a second veal patty. Press around the edges to seal together securely.

In a skillet, combine the oil and 1 tablespoon of the butter over medium-high heat. When the butter melts, add the veal patties. Cook on one side until lightly browned, about 2 minutes. Turn and continue cooking, turning the patties carefully several times so that they cook evenly until done to preference, about 8 minutes in all for medium-rare.

Meanwhile, toast the bread slices.

Place the patties on the bread slices. Heat the remaining 4 tablespoons butter in the skillet, swirling it around until it is hazelnut brown. Sprinkle the patties with the lemon juice. Pour the browned butter over the patties and serve hot.

Serves 4.

Copyright © by Craig Claiborne. Used by permission.

1 pound lean ground veal
1 small yellow onion
¼ cup finely chopped fresh dill or parsley
½ cup fine fresh bread crumbs
¼ cup milk
¼ teaspoon freshly grated nutmeg
Salt
Freshly ground black pepper
4 bread slices, preferably whole wheat
8 thin rounds prosciutto, each about 1½ inches in diameter
8 thin circles Gruyère or other Swiss cheese, each about 1½ inches in diameter
2 tablespoons peanut oil or vegetable oil
5 tablespoons unsalted butter
Juice of ½ lemon

Michael Chiarello's Italian Sausage Burgers

Tra Vigne in St. Helena has long been a destination of mine for Italian-inspired food prepared with California ingredients. Since my move to the Napa Valley, it has become my neighborhood hangout. Chef Michael Chiarello's *panino di calabrese* is destined to become a burger classico. At Tra Vigne, a lightly dressed salad of mixed young greens accompanies the sandwich.

In a small bowl, combine the Mayonnaise with pesto to taste. Set aside, or cover and refrigerate for up to 3 days.

To make the sausage, combine the pork, fennel seed, ground chile, chile flakes to taste, and salt and pepper in a bowl. Mix well, cover, and refrigerate for at least 1 hour or, preferably, overnight for flavors to blend.

In a grill, prepare a hot fire for direct-heat cooking.

Handling the meat as little as possible to avoid compacting it, divide the sausage mixture into 4 equal portions and form the portions into round patties to fit the buns.

When the fire is ready, brush the grill rack with vegetable oil. Place the patties on the grill and cook until browned on the bottom, about 4 minutes. With a wide spatula, turn the patties and cook until done to preference, about 4 minutes longer for medium-rare. During the last few minutes of cooking, place the buns, cut side down, around the outer edges of the grill to toast lightly and top each patty with a slice of the cheese to melt.

Spread the cut sides of the buns with the pesto mayonnaise. Place the grilled peppers on the bottom halves of the buns, top with the patties and the arugula, and cover with the bun tops.

Serves 4.

Copyright © 1992 by Michael Chiarello. Used by permission.

¼ cup Mayonnaise (page 91), made with pure olive oil
Basil pesto (use a favorite recipe)
1 pound coarsely ground pork butt
1 tablespoon fennel seed
2 tablespoons freshly ground dried Anaheim chile, New Mexico chile (also called California chile or *Chile Colorado* when dried), or other moderately hot chiles
Dried chile flakes, preferably from hot New Mexico chiles
2 teaspoons salt
½ teaspoon freshly ground black pepper
4 buns, preferably made from *focaccia* dough (see page 88 or use a favorite recipe)
Vegetable oil for brushing on grill rack
4 slices Italian Fontina cheese
1 red sweet pepper, roasted, peeled, stemmed, seeded, and sliced lengthwise
Tender arugula leaves

Vi Gianaras' Greek Panos' Burgers

2 pounds ground chuck
4 large thick pita breads, or 4 large
    sesame egg buns, split
4 garlic cloves, minced or pressed
4 ounces (1 stick) unsalted butter,
    softened
Vegetable oil for brushing on grill
    rack
1 cup crumbled feta cheese (about
    4 ounces)
2 tablespoons fruity olive oil,
    preferably extra-virgin Greek
½ pound mushrooms, sliced
1 small red onion, thinly sliced
½ cup dry white wine
Salt
Freshly ground black pepper
Green leaf lettuce
Tomato slices

Panos' in San Francisco is my favorite meeting place in my old Noe Valley neighborhood. Vi Gianaras's grill features California-Greek food. I rank her burgers among the very best.

Alternatively, serve the patties between two toasted regular-sized pita breads.

In a grill, prepare a hot fire for direct-heat cooking.

Handling the meat as little as possible to avoid compacting it, divide the chuck into 4 equal portions and form the portions into half-moon-shaped patties to fit one half of each pita bread or into round patties to fit the buns.

In a small bowl, combine the garlic and butter. Spread a little on one side of each pita bread or on the cut sides of the buns. Set aside.

When the fire is ready, brush the grill rack with vegetable oil. Place the patties on the grill and cook until browned on the bottom, about 4 minutes. With a wide spatula, turn the patties and cook until done to preference, about 4 minutes longer for medium-rare. During the last few minutes of cooking, place the pita breads, buttered side down, or the buns, cut side down, on the outer edges of the grill to toast lightly and top each patty with ¼ cup of the cheese to melt.

Meanwhile, in a sauté pan, heat the olive oil on the grill or over high heat on a stove top. Add the mushrooms and onion and sauté for about 1 minute. Add the wine and salt and pepper to taste. Continue sautéing until the vegetables are tender and the liquid is completely evaporated, about 3 minutes. Keep warm.

Place the patties to one side of the buttered side of each pita bread or on the bottom halves of the buns, top with some of the sautéed mushroom mixture, and cover with the bun tops (if used). Serve the lettuce and tomato on the side. To eat on pita, fold the pita bread over to encase the patties.

Serves 4.

Cindy Pawlcyn's Buckeye Burgers

Buckeye Burger Relish (page 90)
42 ounces ground beef
Salt
Freshly ground black pepper
6 hamburger buns, split
Vegetable oil for brushing on grill
    rack
6 slices smoked jack or white Cheddar
    cheese
6 crisp lettuce leaves such as romaine
6 tomato slices (in season)
6 thin sweet red onion slices

Cindy Pawlcyn and partners operate one of California's most successful restaurant groups. Their domain includes Mustards' Grill and Tra Vigne in the Napa Valley, Buckeye Roadhouse in Mill Valley, and Fog City Diner, Roti, and Bix in San Francisco. Cindy claims that her burger is at its best when served on a bun from the estimable Bay Area Acme Bread Company and accompanied with French fries and a malt.

Prepare the relish and set aside.

In a grill, prepare a hot fire for direct-heat cooking.

In a bowl, combine the meat with salt and pepper to taste. Handling the meat as little as possible to avoid compacting it, mix well. Divide the beef into 6 equal portions and form the portions into patties the size and shape of the buns.

When the fire is ready, brush the grill rack with vegetable oil. Place the patties on the grill and cook until browned on the bottom, about 4 minutes. With a wide spatula, turn the patties and cook until done to preference, about 4 minutes longer for medium-rare. During the last few minutes of cooking, place the rolls, cut side down, on the outer edges of the grill to toast lightly and top each patty with a cheese slice to melt.

Place the patties on the bottom halves of the buns, top with lettuce, tomato, onion, and relish, and cover with the bun tops.

Serves 6.

Paul Prudhomme's Bronzed Burgers

The Cajun cooking of southern Louisiana is popular from coast to coast, due in no small measure to the highly creative Paul Prudhomme, chef-owner of K-Paul's in New Orleans. His seasoning blends, such as the one called for in this recipe, are available in most major supermarket chains or directly from Chef Paul Prudhomme (1-800-457-2857).

In a small sauté pan over medium heat, melt the butter. Add the chopped onions and sauté until translucent, about 5 minutes. Reduce the heat and continue to cook until the onions are golden brown, about 15 minutes. (You should end up with about ¾ cup caramelized onion.) Remove from the heat and set aside.

In a large bowl, place the ground meat and sprinkle it with 1 tablespoon of the Meat Magic®. Work the seasoning into the meat with your hands. Then sprinkle the remaining 1 tablespoon Meat Magic® over the meat and again mix well until thoroughly incorporated. Add the caramelized onion to the meat mixture and combine thoroughly. Divide the meat into 6 equal portions and form the portions into patties to fit the buns.

Place a heavy griddle or large, heavy skillet over medium heat and heat to 350° F, about 7 minutes for a gas stove or about 23 minutes for an electric stove. Or preheat an electric skillet to 350° F.

Place as many of the patties as will fit comfortably without crowding on the hot griddle or skillet and cook until browned on the bottom, about 3 minutes. With a wide spatula, turn the patties and cook until done to preference, about 3 minutes longer for medium-rare. Transfer the patties to a plate, then wipe the griddle or skillet thoroughly before cooking the remaining patties in the same manner.

Meanwhile, heat or toast the buns or rolls.

Serve the patties on the buns or rolls and offer the condiments at the table.

Serves 6.

Copyright © 1986 by Paul Prudhomme. Used by permission.

½ cup (½ stick) unsalted butter
2 small yellow onions, coarsely chopped
2 pounds ground chuck, ground round, ground very lean beef, or ground veal
2 tablespoons Chef Paul Prudhomme's Meat Magic®, or to taste
6 hamburger buns or onion rolls, split

CONDIMENTS
Shredded lettuce
Tomato slices
Red onion slices
Mayonnaise (page 91) or high-quality commercial mayonnaise
Creole mustard or Dijon-style mustard
Kosher dill pickle slices

Stephan Pyles' Southwestern Venison Burgers

Stephan Pyles, chef-owner of Routh Street Cafe and Baby Routh in Dallas, Texas, and Goodfellow's and Tejas in Minneapolis, Minnesota, is a leading proponent of modern Southwest cooking.

Prepare the buns and split them. Set aside. Preheat an oven to 400° F.

Cut *ancho* and *chipotle* chiles in half. Remove and discard the seeds and stems and soak the chiles in the wine or water for 1 hour, or until the peppers are saturated. Transfer to a blender with the soaking liquid and purée. Set aside.

While dried chiles are soaking, halve, seed, and stem the *poblanos* and sweet pepper. Place on a lightly oiled baking sheet, skin side up, and roast in the oven until the skin turns light brown, 15 to 20 minutes. Transfer the peppers to a bowl and cover with plastic wrap until cool. When cool, peel and seed the peppers and then cut into small dice.

In a sauté pan or skillet, heat the vegetable oil over medium-high heat. Add the onion and garlic and sauté until translucent, about 5 minutes. Add the cumin and coriander and continue to cook for about 30 seconds. Remove from the heat and let cool to room temperature.

In a grill, prepare a medium-hot fire for direct-heat cooking.

In a meat grinder or food processor, grind the venison and pork fat back together and place in a large bowl. Add the reserved onion-garlic mixture, chile purée, diced peppers, oregano, cilantro, bread crumbs, and egg. Lightly season with salt and pepper. Handling the meat as little as possible to avoid compacting it, mix well. Divide the mixture into 4 equal portions and form the portions into patties to fit the buns. Season the patties with salt and pepper and brush lightly with oil.

When the fire is ready, brush the grill rack with vegetable oil. Place the patties on the grill and cook until browned on the bottom, about 4 minutes. With a wide spatula, turn the patties and cook until done to preference, about 4 minutes longer for medium-rare. During the last few minutes of cooking, place the buns, cut side down, on the outer edges of the grill to toast lightly.

Place the patties on the bottom halves of the buns and cover with the bun tops. Offer the condiments at the table.

Serves 4.

Copyright © 1991 by Stephan Pyles. Used by permission.

Cilantro-Sweet Onion Buns (page 87)
1 dried *ancho* chile
1 dried *chipotle* chile (smoked jalapeño)
¼ cup dry red wine or cold water
2 fresh *poblano* chiles (sometimes sold as *pasilla* chiles)
1 red sweet pepper
2 tablespoons corn oil or other high-quality vegetable oil
½ cup minced yellow onion
2 tablespoons minced or pressed garlic
1 teaspoon ground cumin
2 teaspoons ground coriander
1 pound venison
8 ounces pork fat back
1 teaspoon crumbled dried oregano
1 tablespoon chopped fresh cilantro (coriander)
1 slice stale white bread, broken into fine crumbs
1 egg
Salt
Freshly ground black pepper
Vegetable oil for brushing on the patties and on grill rack

CONDIMENTS
Mayonnaise
Mustard
Catsup

Judy Rodgers' Zuni Burgers

3 pounds beef chuck with about 20
   percent fat, cut into long, thin
   strips
1½ teaspoons sea salt

AÏOLI
2 garlic cloves
1 egg yolk, at room temperature
½ cup olive oil, preferably extra-
   virgin
Salt

Rosemary-scented *focaccia* (see page
   88 or use a favorite recipe or
   purchase from an Italian bakery),
   cut into 5- to 6-inch squares
Vegetable oil for brushing on grill
   rack
Olive oil for brushing on burger

The Zuni Cafe is one of San Francisco's most successful restaurants. The Zuni burger, grilled over oak wood, is a major reason for its popularity among many regular customers, myself included.

Chef Judy Rodgers recommends choosing bright red chuck that has not been stored in Cryo-vac. Zuni burgers may be topped with grilled red onion slices or melted Gorgonzola or Gruyère cheese and are always served with turmeric-flavored zucchini pickles (made from a *Joy of Cooking* recipe) and red onions that have been pickled in distilled vinegar with sugar, cinnamon, bay, chile, allspice, star anise, and peppercorns.

In a bowl, toss the meat with the salt. Cover and refrigerate overnight.

To make the aïoli, chop the garlic in a food processor or blender. Add the egg yolk and blend well. With the motor running, drizzle in the oil and blend until smooth and thick. Season to taste with salt. Cover and refrigerate for at least 1 hour or as long as overnight. Return to room temperature before serving.

No more than 6 hours before cooking the burgers, grind the meat in a meat grinder or food processor. Handling the meat as little as possible to avoid compacting it, divide the beef into 6 equal portions and form the portions into round patties to fit the *focaccia* squares.

In a grill, prepare a hot fire for direct-heat cooking.

When the fire is ready, brush the grill rack with vegetable oil and brush patties lightly with the olive oil. Place the patties on the grill and cook until browned on the bottom, about 4 minutes. With a wide spatula, turn the patties and cook until done to preference, about 4 minutes longer for medium-rare. A few minutes before the burgers are ready, slice the *focaccia* in half horizontally and place the slices, cut side down, on the outer edges of the grill to toast lightly.

Spread the bottom halves of the *focaccia* with the aïoli, add the patties, and cover with the tops.

Serves 6.

Anne Rosenzweig's Arcadia Burgers

Creative American chef Anne Rosenzweig's burger for the "21" Club in New York received much acclaim from the food press. The 12-ounce "21" burger costs over $21 by the way. The burger served in her Arcadia restaurant deserves equal praise.

Anne serves her giant burgers with fried waffle-cut potatoes and "no catsup."

In a bowl or mini food processor, combine the butter, basil, thyme, and parsley and blend well. Lightly season with salt and pepper. Form into a log about 1 inch in diameter, roll in plastic wrap, and freeze until firm.

In a grill, prepare a medium fire for direct-heat cooking.

Handling the meat as little as possible to avoid compacting it, divide the beef into 4 equal portions and form the portions into balls. Make an indentation in each ball and press 1 tablespoon of the frozen herb butter into the meat. Bring the meat together to encase the butter in the center and form the balls into patties the size and shape of the bread slices. Sprinkle the patties on both sides with salt and pepper to taste.

When the fire is ready, brush the grill rack with vegetable oil. Place the patties on the grill and cook until browned on the bottom, about 4 minutes. With a wide spatula, turn the patties and cook until done to preference, about 4 minutes longer for medium-rare. During the last few minutes of cooking, brush each bread slice on one side only with 1 tablespoon olive oil. Place the slices, oiled side down, on the outer edges of the grill to toast lightly, then turn and toast on the other side.

In a bowl, combine the tomato and onion slices. Sprinkle with the remaining ½ cup olive oil, the lemon juice, and salt and pepper to taste. Toss gently.

Place 4 of the bread slices, oiled side up, on serving plates and top with the patties. Cover with the remaining bread slices, oiled side down. Offer the tomato-onion salad as a condiment.

Serves 4.

Copyright © 1986 by Anne Rosenzweig. Used by permission.

¼ cup (½ stick) unsalted butter, at room temperature
1 tablespoon finely chopped fresh basil
1½ teaspoons finely chopped fresh thyme
1½ teaspoons finely chopped fresh parsley
Salt
Freshly ground black pepper
3 pounds ground chuck (20 to 22 percent fat content)
8 slices Italian peasant bread, about 5 inches in diameter and ½ inch thick
Vegetable oil for brushing on grill rack
¾ cup olive oil, preferably extra-virgin
8 to 12 tomato slices
8 thin red onion slices
2 tablespoons plus 2 teaspoons freshly squeezed lemon juice

Jimmy Schmidt's Spicy Rattle Burgers with Chiles

1½ pounds beef chuck, trimmed and cubed
8 ounces sirloin fat trimmings, cubed
2 large egg yolks
½ teaspoon salt
½ teaspoon freshly ground black pepper
2 dried or canned *chipotle* chiles (smoked jalapeños), stemmed and minced
1 fresh *poblano* pepper, roasted, peeled, stemmed, seeded, and cut into small squares
1 red sweet pepper, roasted, peeled, stemmed, seeded, and cut into small squares
4 great burger buns, split
Vegetable oil for brushing on cooking surface
4 thick sweet onion slices
Olive oil for brushing on onion
1 bunch arugula, trimmed
4 skewers assorted pickle chunks, pickled peppers, pickled onions, and other pickled vegetables for garnish

CONDIMENTS
Mayonnaise
Mustard
Catsup

Chef-owner Jimmy Schmidt rose to national acclaim with his Rattlesnake Club in Denver. This recipe comes from his restaurant in Detroit, where he also operates Tres Vita and Cocina del Sol.

Place the chuck, fat, and a meat grinder in a freezer for 1 hour.

Force the chilled beef and fat through the large disc of the grinder into a large bowl. Mix in the egg yolks, then force the mixture through the medium disc of the meat grinder into another bowl. With your fingertips, fold in the salt, pepper, *chipotle* and *poblano* chiles, and sweet pepper. Handling the meat as little as possible to avoid compacting it, divide the beef mixture into 4 equal portions and form the portions into patties to fit the buns. Refrigerate until ready to cook.

In a grill, prepare a hot fire for indirect-heat cooking, or preheat a broiler until very hot.

When the grill or broiler is ready, brush the grill or broiler rack with vegetable oil. Place the patties on the grill or broiler rack and cook until browned on the bottom, about 4 minutes. Using a wide spatula, turn the patties, then raise the grate on the grill, move the patties to a cooler spot on the grill, or lower the temperature on the broiler. Cook the burgers until done to preference, about 4 minutes longer for medium-rare. Meanwhile, brush the onion slices with oil and grill or broil alongside the burgers, turning several times, until tender, about 5 minutes. Remove the patties to a platter and allow to rest about 3 minutes before serving to allow the juices to settle. (Do not stack them on top of each other!)

While the burgers are resting, grill or toast the buns.

Place the patties on the bottom halves of the buns. Top with the grilled onion and arugula. Garnish each plate with a skewer of mixed pickles. Offer the condiments at the table.

Serves 4.

Copyright © 1991 by Jimmy Schmidt. Used by permission.

Jeremiah Tower's Truffled Stars Burgers

Stars is one of San Francisco's hottest tickets. Owner-chef Jeremiah Tower states that "Hamburgers are best in English muffins, a baguette, or a firm, dense hamburger roll. The bread must be buttered and toasted for that final sensual push. The fitting drink with this sandwich, and one without which the burger falls short of its overwhelming effect, is a luscious, old-fashioned, deep red, rich, and powerful Burgundy—a La Tache, any wine made by Roumier (his own or Comte de Vogue), or a Morey-Saint-Denis—in a large balloon glass, so the perfume of the wine and the truffled beef hit one's brain at the same time."

Finely chop the truffle. Stir one fourth of it into the mayonnaise, cover, and refrigerate for a few hours.

In a bowl, lightly mix the remaining chopped truffle into the beef by hand. Cover loosely and let stand at room temperature for 4 hours, so that the truffle perfume permeates the meat.

Season the truffled burger meat with salt and pepper to taste. Handling the meat as little as possible to avoid compacting it, divide the beef into 4 equal portions and form the portions into patties, making neat edges, to fit the muffins.

In a grill, prepare a hot fire for direct-heat cooking, or preheat a heavy skillet or griddle until very hot.

When the grill rack, skillet, or griddle is ready, brush it with vegetable oil. Grill or pancook the patties until browned on the bottom, about 4 minutes, seasoning them a little more with salt and pepper on the outside as they cook. With a wide spatula, turn the patties and cook until done to preference, about 4 minutes longer for medium-rare.

Meanwhile, toast or grill the muffins, then butter each half.

Transfer the burgers to the bottom halves of the muffins. Spoon 1 tablespoon of the truffled mayonnaise on top of each burger and cover them with the muffin tops.

Serves 4.

Copyright © 1991 by Jeremiah Tower. Used by permission.

1 fresh black truffle (about 2 ounces)
¼ cup mayonnaise, preferably homemade (see page 91 or use a favorite recipe)
2 pounds ground beef chuck or ground sirloin (22 percent fat if using a charcoal grill, or only 18 percent fat if using a flat-top griddle or heavy skillet)
About 2 teaspoons salt
About 1 teaspoon freshly ground black pepper
4 English muffins (Thomas type), split
Vegetable oil for brushing on cooking surface
3 tablespoons butter

Barbara Tropp's China Moon Cafe Wonton Burgers

¼ cup plus 2 tablespoons sliced green onion, including some green tops
¼ cup chopped fresh Chinese chives or cilantro (coriander)
1½ tablespoons finely minced fresh ginger root
2½ tablespoons finely minced garlic
¼ cup plus 1 tablespoon soy sauce
1½ tablespoons Chinese rice wine or dry sherry
1½ teaspoons coarse kosher salt
1 teaspoon finely ground black pepper
1½ tablespoons hot chile oil
¼ cup unsalted homemade chicken stock or canned low-sodium chicken broth
3 pounds coarsely ground pork butt (use about 1 part fat to 3 to 4 parts lean)
2 slender French baguettes, each cut crosswise into 4 equal portions and then split lengthwise
Peanut oil or corn oil
Dijon-style mustard

Burgers made from leftover spicy pork wonton filling is a favorite staff lunch at China Moon Cafe in San Francisco. The meat mixture is moist and zestily seasoned, so a mild Dijon mustard is a terrific accompaniment, or serve with China Moon Sesame Mustard (page 91). Chef-owner Barbara Tropp states that "all of this is a bit zany, but then so is the idea of a wonton burger!"

Wonton, by the way, translates as "cosmic chaos." The word dates back to Chinese antiquity when the universe was described as a jumble of light and dark enclosed in a thin shell, hence the edible invention of the wonton.

Any favorite bread may be substituted for the baguettes. Just shape the meat mixture to match the bread.

In a large bowl, combine the green onion, chives or cilantro, ginger, garlic, soy sauce, rice wine or sherry, salt, pepper, chile oil, and stock or broth and mix well. Add the pork and stir in one direction with your hands or a large spoon just until the mixture is thoroughly blended. Do not overwork the meat. (At this point the mixture can be sealed airtight and refrigerated overnight. The flavors will actually enlarge. Bring to room temperature before cooking.)

Handling the meat mixture as little as possible to avoid compacting it, divide it into 8 equal portions and form the portions into rectangles to fit the bread. Brush a heavy skillet with a film of peanut oil or corn oil. Remember that the pork will render some of its own fat, so you'll need only minimal oil for cooking. Place the pan over high heat and heat it as hot as possible. Add the patties and sear, turning once, until well browned on both sides. Reduce the heat and cook until done to your preference. If you are concerned about underdone pork, use an instant-read thermometer and cook the burgers to the government-approved internal temperature of 160° F; the meat will still be pink and moist.

Spread the cut surfaces of the baguette portions with mustard and enclose the patties inside.

Serves 8.

Copyright © 1991 by Barbara Tropp. Used by permission.

Alice Waters' Chez Panisse Burgers

About 1½ pounds ground beef chuck,
    preferably naturally raised
Salt
Freshly ground black pepper
Finely chopped garlic, plus 1 garlic
    clove, cut in half
4 soft sandwich rolls, split, or
    8 country-style bread slices
Olive oil for brushing on cooking
    surface and for drizzling on rolls
    or bread
Red onion slices
Dijon-style mustard
Spicy greens such as lovage, arugula,
    and watercress
Tomato slices (optional)

Alice Waters, the *grande dame* of the new American cooking, believes that "a hamburger is as much about bread as it is about meat. The ratio of meat to bread must be right—*i.e.,* the volume of the two pieces of bread should be roughly equal to the ground meat. Also, the bread or roll should be soft enough to blend with the meat." Alice prefers a country bread with a fairly thin crust, cut into slices thick enough to hold together during toasting and to survive dripping meat juices.

Alice serves good dill pickles on the side, with a few thickly cut French fries and a glass of Gigondas.

In a bowl, combine the chuck with salt, pepper, and chopped garlic to taste. Handling the meat mixture as little as possible to avoid compacting it, mix well. Divide the beef into 4 equal portions and form the portions into patties to fit the bread.

In a grill, prepare a hot charcoal fire for direct-heat cooking or preheat a cast-iron skillet to very hot.

When the grill or skillet is ready, brush the cooking surface with olive oil. Grill or pancook the patties until browned on the bottom, about 4 minutes. With a wide spatula, turn the patties and cook until done to preference, about 4 minutes longer for medium-rare. Cook the onion slices at the same time, turning frequently, until tender, about 5 minutes.

Meanwhile, toast or grill the rolls or bread slices until golden brown. Generously rub the toasted rolls or bread with the cut sides of the halved garlic clove and drizzle with olive oil. Spread the cut sides of the roll bottoms or half of the bread slices with mustard.

Transfer the patties to the mustard-spread rolls or bread and crown with the onion. Pile the greens on the remaining halves of the rolls or bread slices and add tomato (if used). Present the burgers open-face.

Serves 4.

ACCOMPANIMENTS

Great burgers taste even better when served on fresh-from-the-oven breads that are slathered with your own homemade condiments and relishes. And what are burgers without crisp pickles and great fries?

Whole-Wheat
Hamburger Buns

For a lighter bun, replace the whole-wheat flour with all-purpose flour, or use two parts whole wheat to one part white flour. You may also use any favorite bread recipe and follow the directions for forming buns detailed below.

As with most breads, these buns are best eaten the day they are baked. If you don't plan to use them all, some of the dough can be frozen. After the second rising, the dough can be divided into individual portions, wrapped tightly in plastic freezer wrap, and frozen for up to two months. Defrost, allow to rise, and bake as directed.

1 tablespoon sugar
⅓ cup warm water (105° to 110° F)
1 envelope (scant 1 tablespoon or ¼ ounce) active dry yeast
About 3½ cups whole-wheat flour
1½ teaspoons salt
1 egg, lightly beaten
1 cup lukewarm water or milk
5 tablespoons unsalted butter
Vegetable oil or softened unsalted butter for greasing bowl and baking sheet
1 egg, lightly beaten, for wash

OPTIONAL TOPPINGS
Coarse salt
Freshly cracked black pepper
Caraway seeds
Poppy seeds
Sesame seeds

In a small bowl, dissolve the sugar (which "feeds" the yeast) in the warm water. Sprinkle the yeast over the water and stir gently until it dissolves. Let stand in a warm place until a thin layer of foam covers the surface, about 5 minutes, indicating that the yeast is effective. (Discard mixture and start over with fresh yeast if bubbles have not formed within 5 minutes.)

To mix and knead the dough by hand, combine 3 cups of the flour and the salt in a large mixing bowl and stir well. Make a well in the center of the flour and pour in the yeast mixture, egg, and lukewarm water or milk. Vigorously stir the flour into the liquid to form a soft dough. Turn the dough out onto a flour-dusted surface and knead for about 10 minutes. Place the 5 tablespoons butter on the side of the work surface and knead it into the dough a little at a time. Continue kneading until the dough is soft, smooth, and elastic, about 10 minutes longer. At this point, if the dough is too sticky, add more flour, a little at a time, and knead until the dough is the proper consistency.

To mix and knead the dough in a heavy-duty standing electric mixer, install the flat beater. Add 3 cups of the flour and the salt and mix well. Add the yeast mixture, egg, and lukewarm water or milk and mix at medium speed for about 1 minute. Replace the flat beater with a dough hook and knead at medium speed for 2 minutes. Cut the butter into small pieces and begin to add it a little at a time while continuing to knead until the dough is soft, smooth, and elastic, about 3 minutes longer. If the dough is too sticky, add more flour, a little at a time, and beat until the dough is the proper consistency.

After mixing the dough by one of the above methods, shape the dough into a ball and place it in a well-greased bowl, turning to coat completely on all sides with the oil or butter. Cover the bowl tightly with plastic wrap to prevent moisture loss and set aside in a warm, draft-free place (75° to 85° F—a warmer environment may kill the yeast) until doubled in bulk, 1½ to 2 hours.

Gently punch down the dough to release the gas. Form the dough into a smooth ball again, return it to the bowl, cover, and set aside to rise again until doubled in bulk, about half as long as the first rising.

Cilantro-Sweet Onion Buns

Turn the dough out onto a floured surface, keeping the smooth top upright. Using a flour-dusted rolling pin or floured hands, begin at one side and work to the other to press out the air. Divide the dough into 6 equal portions. Using your hands, shape each piece of dough into a smooth round ball, then gently flatten each ball out with your hand or a rolling pin to form a disc about the diameter you want the cooked bun to be; they rise up, not out. Avoid tearing the smooth top of the buns when flattening them. Place the buns on a parchment-lined or greased baking sheet, cover with a damp towel, and set in a warm, draft-free place until doubled in size, about 30 minutes.

Preheat an oven to 400° F.

Brush the tops of the buns with the egg wash. Sprinkle the buns with one or a combination of the toppings. Position the baking sheet in the top half of the oven and bake until the buns are golden brown all over, about 20 minutes. Transfer the baking sheet to a wire rack and let cool for about 10 minutes. Remove the buns from the pan to the rack and let cool completely.

Makes 6 buns.

Stephan Pyles serves venison burgers on these buns at his Routh Street Cafe and Baby Routh in Dallas. You will need a heavy-duty electric mixer with a whip attachment and a dough hook to make these delectable little breads.

1 envelope (scant 1 tablespoon or ¼ ounce) active dry yeast
¼ cup sugar
3 cups all-purpose flour
¾ cup warm water (105° to 110° F)
2 eggs, lightly beaten
¼ cup unsalted butter, melted and cooled
1½ teaspoons salt
½ sweet onion such as Noonday, Texas Spring Sweet, Walla Walla, or Vidalia, cut into very fine dice
2 tablespoons chopped fresh cilantro (coriander)
Vegetable oil or butter for greasing bowl
1 egg, lightly beaten, for wash

In the bowl of an electric mixer, whisk together the yeast, sugar, and ¾ cup of the flour. Let stand for 2 to 3 minutes. Add the water, eggs, and butter and beat with the whip attachment, scraping down the sides of the bowl occasionally, until smooth, about 3 minutes.

Replace the whip with the dough hook. Add the salt, onion, cilantro, and the remaining flour, ¾ cup at a time, and knead until a soft dough forms that easily pulls away from the sides of the bowl. The dough should be a little sticky.

Shape the dough into a ball and place it in a well-greased bowl, turning to coat completely on all sides with the oil or butter. Cover the bowl tightly with plastic wrap and place in a warm, draft-free area until doubled in bulk, about 1½ hours.

Gently punch down the dough and turn it out onto a lightly floured surface. Divide the dough into 6 equal portions and form each into a bun shape. Arrange the buns on a baking sheet, cover with a damp towel, and place in a warm, draft-free place until doubled in size, about half as long as the first rising.

Preheat an oven to 375° F.

Slash the top of each bun once with a razor blade and brush the buns with the egg wash. Bake until golden brown, 20 to 25 minutes. Transfer the baking sheet to a wire rack and let cool for 8 to 10 minutes. Remove the buns from the pan to the rack and let cool completely.

Makes 6 buns.

Copyright © 1991 by Stephan Pyles.
Used by permission.

Herbed Italian Flat Hearth Bread (Focaccia)

Wonderful as a substitute for old-fashioned hamburger buns. Traditional recipes call for long kneading by hand; I've shortened the process by using a food processor or a large stationery electric mixer.

1 tablespoon sugar
1 cup warm water (105° to 110° F)
1 envelope (scant 1 tablespoon or ¼ ounce) active dry yeast, or 1 ounce fresh yeast cake
¼ cup fruity olive oil, preferably extra-virgin, plus extra oil for oiling bowl and baking pan and for brushing on unbaked bread
1 teaspoon salt
About 4 cups all-purpose flour
About 2 tablespoons minced fresh sage or rosemary, or 1 tablespoon crumbled dried sage or rosemary, or to taste
Coarse salt

In a small bowl, dissolve the sugar in the warm water. Sprinkle the yeast over the water and stir gently until it dissolves. Let stand in a warm place until a thin layer of foam forms on the surface, about 5 minutes.

In a food processor or the bowl of a heavy-duty electric mixer, combine the ¼ cup oil, salt, 3 cups of the flour, and the foamy yeast. Beat at medium speed until the dough is elastic. Add about ½ cup more of the flour and beat until the dough is stiff.

Transfer the dough to a lightly floured work surface and knead until smooth and elastic, adding as much of the remaining ½ cup flour as necessary to make a dough that is not sticky.

Shape the dough into a ball and place in a well-oiled bowl, turning to coat completely on all sides. Cover the bowl tightly with plastic wrap and let rise in a warm, draft-free place until doubled in size, from 1 to 3 hours.

Preheat an oven to 450° F. Grease an 11-by-15-inch shallow baking pan.

Gently punch down the dough and roll it out on a lightly floured work surface to form a rectangle that will fit into the prepared pan. Pat the dough evenly into the pan. Cover and let rise for 30 minutes.

With your fingertips, make indentions about 1 inch apart all over the surface of the dough. Brush the dough with olive oil, then sprinkle with the sage or rosemary and salt to taste.

Bake until golden brown, about 15 minutes. Cut into 6 squares, then split in half horizontally and serve hot. Or cool the bread to room temperature, cut into squares, and grill or toast just before using.

Makes six 5-inch squares.

VARIATIONS. During kneading, add one or more of the following to the dough: 2 tablespoons or more minced or pressed garlic; 3 tablespoons drained and minced sun-dried tomatoes packed in olive oil; 6 slices crisply cooked bacon, crumbled; 2 tablespoons dried chile flakes or ground dried chile; ½ cup freshly grated Parmesan cheese; ½ cup pizza sauce or tomato sauce. Adjust amounts to taste.

Bread-and-Butter Pickles

Whether made from cucumbers or summer squash, these spicy, sweet pickles are great on burgers.

2 quarts distilled white vinegar of 4 to 6 percent acidity
4 cups sugar
6 tablespoons salt
4 teaspoons celery seeds
4 teaspoons dill seeds
1 tablespoon ground turmeric
2 teaspoons dry mustard
4 quarts thinly sliced pickling cucumber or zucchini (about 5 pounds)
1 quart thinly sliced white onion (3 or 4 large onions)

In a saucepan, combine the vinegar, sugar, salt, celery seeds, dill seeds, turmeric, and mustard. Bring to a boil over medium-high heat. Mix the cucumber or zucchini and onion slices in a ceramic bowl, pour the vinegar mixture over the top, and let stand at room temperature for 1 hour.

Sterilize pint canning jars, new lids, rings, and all the utensils in boiling water for 15 minutes. Using tongs, remove the jars and place upside down on paper toweling to drain. Remove the remaining equipment and place on toweling as well.

Kosher-Style Dill Pickles

Transfer the vegetable mixture to a large pot over medium-high heat. Bring to a boil and cook for 3 minutes. Pack immediately into the hot, sterilized jars, allowing about ¼ inch head room. Wipe jar rim threads clean with paper toweling, cover with lids, and tighten rings. Place the jars on a rack in a large pot filled with enough boiling water to cover the jar tops by at least 2 inches. Return the water to a boil, cover, and let jars stand in the boiling water for 10 minutes.

With a jar lifter, lift each jar straight up out of the water bath. Place jars on a countertop and let stand undisturbed until cold. Check the seal on the lids after 24 hours; the lids should be slightly depressed. Store any jars that did not seal properly in the refrigerator and use their contents as soon as possible. Store sealed jars in a cool, dark, dry place for at least 1 week before eating. Refrigerate after opening.

Makes 6 to 7 pints.

If small cucumbers are not available, use larger ones and allow twice as long for water-bath processing. Or cut large cucumbers into halves, quarters, or slices and process as for small ones.

3 quarts pickling cucumbers, preferably no larger than 4 inches long (about 4 pounds)
6 fresh dill heads, or 6 teaspoons dill seeds
3 tablespoons mixed pickling spices
6 garlic cloves
3 cups distilled white vinegar
3 cups water
6 tablespoons salt

Wash the cucumbers, scrubbing thoroughly.

Sterilize pint or quart canning jars, new lids, rings, and all the utensils in boiling water for 15 minutes. Using tongs, remove the jars and place upside down on paper toweling to drain. Remove the remaining equipment and place on toweling as well.

Pack the cucumbers into the hot, sterilized jars. If using pint jars, add 1 fresh dill head or 1 teaspoon dill seeds, 1½ teaspoons pickling spices, and 1 garlic clove to each jar; double the amounts for quart jars.

In a saucepan, combine the vinegar, water, and salt over high heat. Bring to a boil. Pour some of the vinegar mixture into each jar, allowing about ¼ inch head room in each pint jar or ½ inch head room in each quart jar. Cover the jars with sterilized lids and screw on the jar rings.

Process in a boiling water bath according to directions for Bread-and-Butter Pickles (preceding), allowing 5 minutes for pint jars or 10 minutes for quart jars, or as directed by jar manufacturer.

Continuing to follow directions, remove from water bath, cool, and check seals. Store sealed jars in a cool, dark, dry place. Pickles will be ready to eat in 4 to 8 weeks. Refrigerate after opening.

Makes 6 pints or 3 quarts.

Buckeye Burger Relish

Chef Cindy Pawlcyn of the Buckeye Roadhouse in Mill Valley, California, tops burgers with this old-fashioned mixture. It keeps in the refrigerator for about three weeks.

3 firm but ripe tomatoes, stemmed, cored, and peeled
¼ head cabbage, cored
2 fresh jalapeño chiles or other hot chiles, stemmed and seeded
2 yellow onions
2 cups rice vinegar
2 cups cider vinegar
1¼ cups sugar
2 teaspoons Dijon-style mustard
1 teaspoon celery seeds
1 teaspoon ground cinnamon
1½ teaspoons ground turmeric

Using a sharp knife, finely chop the tomatoes, cabbage, chiles, and onions. Alternatively, cut the vegetables into chunks, combine them in a food processor fitted with a metal blade, and pulse until roughly chopped.

In a heavy-bottomed saucepan, combine the vegetables with all the remaining ingredients. Place over medium-high heat and bring to a boil. Reduce the heat to low and simmer, uncovered, until thick, 45 minutes to 1 hour; watch carefully to prevent burning.

Remove the pan from the heat and let the relish cool to room temperature. Transfer to jars, cover tightly, and refrigerate.

Makes about 1 quart.

Copyright © 1992 by Cindy Pawlcyn. Used by permission.

Mother's Pear Relish

My mother makes this relish in great quantity each year. She and Daddy enjoy it on venison burgers.

4 pounds firm ripe pears, peeled and cored
2½ pounds yellow onions
3 or 4 green sweet peppers, stemmed and seeded
2 red sweet peppers, stemmed and seeded
3 fresh jalapeño chiles or other hot chiles, stemmed and seeded, or to taste
2 cups sugar
3 tablespoons dry mustard
2½ tablespoons salt
1 tablespoon ground turmeric
3 cups cider vinegar

In a food grinder fitted with a medium disc, grind the pears into a bowl. Using the same disc, grind the onions, sweet peppers, and chiles and add to the pears. Set aside.

Alternatively, chop the pears and vegetables in a food processor.

In a large pot, combine the sugar, mustard, salt, and turmeric. Stir in the vinegar, place over high heat, and stir until the sugar dissolves, about 4 minutes.

Add the ground pear mixture to the vinegar mixture. Bring to a boil, then reduce the heat to low and simmer, uncovered, until the onion is tender but still crisp and most of the liquid evaporates, 30 to 45 minutes.

Sterilize pint canning jars, new lids, rings, and all the utensils in boiling water for 15 minutes. Using tongs, remove the jars and place upside down on paper toweling to drain. Remove the remaining equipment and place on toweling as well.

Pour the pear mixture into the hot, sterilized jars, allowing about ¼ inch head room. Cover the jars with sterilized lids and screw on jar rings. Process in a boiling water bath according to directions for Bread-and-Butter Pickles (page 88) for 5 minutes, or as directed by jar manufacturer.

Continuing to follow directions, remove from water bath and check seals. Store sealed jars in a cool, dark, dry place. Relish is ready to eat immediately. Refrigerate after opening.

Makes 6 pints.

Mayonnaise

For some of us a burger isn't a burger without a bit of this creamy spread.

1 whole egg, at room temperature
1 egg yolk, at room temperature
1 teaspoon Dijon-style mustard
About 2 tablespoons freshly squeezed lemon juice
1 cup high-quality vegetable oil
About ½ teaspoon salt
About ¼ teaspoon freshly ground white pepper

In a blender or food processor, combine the egg, egg yolk, mustard, and 1 tablespoon of the lemon juice; blend for about 30 seconds. With the motor running at high speed, slowly drizzle in the oil in a steady stream and blend until a thick mayonnaise consistency forms. Turn the motor off.

With a rubber or plastic spatula, scrape down any oil from the sides of the container and blend into the mayonnaise. Add salt, pepper, and more lemon juice to taste. Use immediately or transfer to a covered container and refrigerate for up to 2 days.

Makes about 1½ cups.

Mayonnaise Variations

GARLIC MAYONNAISE. Add 2 to 4 garlic cloves when blending the eggs.

HERBED MAYONNAISE. Stir ½ to 1 cup minced fresh herbs into the completed mayonnaise. Use only one herb or a complementary combination. Basil, dill, and tarragon impart their unique flavors and should be used alone or in combination with milder herbs such as chervil or parsley.

ITALIAN *MAIONESE.* Omit the mustard and substitute extra-virgin olive oil for the vegetable oil.

SESAME MAYONNAISE. Add 1 tablespoon soy sauce, or to taste, when blending the eggs. Substitute 3 tablespoons Asian-style sesame oil for 3 tablespoons of the vegetable oil and season to taste with Asian-style hot chile oil.

SPICY MAYONNAISE. Add 1 teaspoon chopped canned *chipotle* chiles packed in *adobo* sauce, or to taste, when blending the eggs.

TANGY MAYONNAISE. Combine equal parts finished mayonnaise and sour cream.

TOMATO MAYONNAISE. Add about 6 sun-dried tomatoes packed in oil, drained and coarsely chopped, when blending the eggs

TRUFFLED MAYONNAISE. Stir as much minced black or white truffle, preferably fresh, into the finished mayonnaise as your taste and budget allow.

China Moon Sesame Mustard

A mild and seductively seasoned mustard for burgers and sandwiches that keeps indefinitely when refrigerated. If the sauce separates, rewhisk to emulsify.

½ cup unflavored Dijon-style mustard, preferably Maille brand
½ cup Japanese sesame oil, preferably Kadoya brand
2 tablespoons unseasoned Japanese rice vinegar
1 tablespoon Chinese rice wine or dry sherry
Fine sea salt

Combine all the ingredients, including salt to taste, and whisk to emulsify.

Makes about 1 cup.

Spicy Tomato Catsup

If you enjoy ketchup on your burgers or fries, try this spicy variation, which is a cross between a chile sauce and catsup.

4 quarts tomatoes, peeled, seeded, and coarsely chopped (about 8 pounds)
2 cups coarsely chopped yellow onion
3 cups coarsely chopped, stemmed, and seeded red sweet peppers
1 cup coarsely chopped, stemmed, and seeded fresh jalapeño chiles or other hot chiles
3 cups distilled white vinegar
1 cup sugar, or more to taste
About 2 tablespoons salt
2 tablespoons celery seeds
1 tablespoon mustard seeds
1 tablespoon whole black peppercorns, lightly crushed
2 teaspoons whole allspice
1 teaspoon whole cloves
4 thin slices fresh ginger root
2 cinnamon sticks, each about 3 inches long
2 bay leaves
Ground cayenne pepper

In a large pot, combine the tomatoes, onion, sweet peppers, and chiles. Bring to a boil over high heat, then reduce the heat to low and simmer until the vegetables are soft, about 30 minutes.

Working in batches, transfer the vegetables to a food processor or blender and purée until smooth.

Return the puréed vegetables to a clean pot. Stir in the vinegar and sugar and salt to taste. Tie the celery seed, mustard seed, peppercorns, allspice, cloves, ginger, cinnamon, and bay leaves in a cheesecloth bag. Add to the mixture. Bring to a boil over high heat, then reduce the heat to low, and simmer, uncovered, until thick, 1 to 2 hours. Stir frequently to prevent sticking. Season to taste with salt and cayenne pepper.

Sterilize pint canning jars, new lids, rings, and all the utensils in boiling water for 15 minutes. Using tongs, remove the jars and place upside down on paper toweling to drain. Remove the remaining equipment and drain on toweling as well.

Pack the tomato mixture into the hot, sterilized jars, allowing about ¼ inch head room. Cover jars with sterilized lids and screw on jar rings. Process in a boiling water bath according to directions for Bread-and-Butter Pickles (page 88), or as directed by jar manufacturer.

Continuing to follow directions, remove from water bath, cool, and check seals. Store sealed jars in a cool, dark, dry place. Catsup is ready to eat immediately. Refrigerate after opening.

Makes 6 to 8 pints.

Tart Cherry Catsup

This alternative to tomato catsup was served by Julie Winter, a finalist in the Sutter Home Build A Better Burger cookoff.

1 cup dried seeded tart cherries
2 cups water, boiling
6 tablespoons red wine vinegar
¼ cup tomato paste
¼ cup finely chopped green onion, white portion only
2 tablespoons sugar

In a bowl, cover the cherries with the boiling water and let stand until the cherries are softened, about 30 minutes. Drain, reserving water.

In a food processor or blender, combine the cherries, ½ cup of the reserved soaking water, and all the remaining ingredients. Purée until smooth. Use immediately, or cover and refrigerate for up to several weeks.

Makes about 1 cup.

French Fries

When cooking more than one batch of potatoes, transfer each batch of fries to a baking sheet lined with several thicknesses of paper toweling and keep warm in a preheated 200° F oven until all the fries are cooked.

Baking potatoes or sweet potatoes (allow 1 medium-sized potato per person)
Canola oil or other high-quality vegetable oil for deep-frying
Salt

Peel the potatoes and cut them into desired shape. Be sure all pieces are about the same size. Rinse in cold water and pat completely dry with paper toweling. Or spin in a salad dryer, then finish drying with paper toweling.

Pour the oil into a deep-fat fryer or deep pan to a depth of about 2 inches. Place the pan over medium heat or heat the electric fryer until the temperature reaches 325° F.

Transfer the drained potatoes to a fry basket and slowly immerse the basket into the hot fat. Alternatively, carefully drop potatoes by handfuls into the hot fat; avoid overcrowding the pan. Cook until the potatoes are soft but not beginning to turn golden, about 3 minutes for thin cuts to about 5 minutes for thick cuts. Remove from the fat (with a slotted utensil if not using a basket), transfer to paper toweling, and let drain for at least 5 minutes or for up to several hours.

Shortly before serving, reheat the cooking fat to 375° to 395° F. Return the potatoes to the hot fat and fry until crisp and golden, about 2 minutes for very thin cuts to about 5 minutes for thick cuts. Drain briefly on paper toweling to remove surface grease. Sprinkle with salt to taste and serve hot.

One medium-sized potato makes 1 serving.

Potato or Other Vegetable Chips

Use a variety of vegetables for a colorful array of fresh chips.

Canola oil or other high-quality vegetable oil for deep-frying
6 cups thinly sliced potato, peeled beet, carrot, peeled lotus root, summer squash, peeled winter squash, peeled sweet potato, or a combination
Salt

In a deep-fat fryer or deep pan, pour in the oil to a depth of about 2 inches. Heat to 375° F. Add the potatoes or other vegetables in batches and cook, stirring frequently, until crisp, 5 to 10 minutes, depending upon thickness; avoid overcrowding the pan. Remove with a slotted utensil to paper toweling to drain. Cook the remaining vegetables, allowing the oil to return to 375° F before adding more vegetables.

Sprinkle the chips with salt to taste. Serve warm or at room temperature.

Serves 4.

RECIPE INDEX

Alice Waters' Chez Panisse Burgers 82
Anne Rosenzweig's Arcadia Burgers 75
Arcadia Burgers 75
Asian Burgers 14

Bacon Cheeseburgers 15
Barbara Tropp's China Moon Cafe
    Wonton Burgers 80
Barbecued Chicken Burgers 24
Basic Burgers 13
Basil-Smoked Burgers, Napa Valley 32
Bean Burgers, Hearty Southern 51
Bread-and-Butter Pickles 89
Bronzed Burgers 65
Buckeye Burger Relish 90
Buckeye Burgers 66
Buns, Cilantro-Sweet Onion 87
Buns, Whole-Wheat Hamburger 86

Calypso Burgers 44
Caribbean Burgers 14
Catahoula Parish Venison Burgers with
    Pear Relish 16
Catsup, Spicy Tomato 92
Catsup, Tart Cherry 92
Cheeseburgers 14
Cherry Catsup, Tart 92
Chez Panisse Burgers 82
Chili Burgers 19
China Moon Burgers 80
China Moon Sesame Mustard 91
Christy Hill Burgers 58
Cilantro-Mint Chutney 35
Cilantro-Sweet Onion Buns 87
Cindy Pawlcyn's Buckeye Burgers 66
Confetti Salsa 43
Craig Claiborne's Veal Burgers Cordon
    Bleu 61
Cranberry-Glazed Turkey Burgers 27

Eggplant Salsa 36

Focaccia 88
Foxy Loxburgers 48
French Burgers 14

Garlic Mayonnaise 91
German Burger 14

Hamburger Buns, Whole-Wheat 86
Hazelnut-Crusted Lamb Burgers 38
Hearty Southern Bean Burgers 51
Herbed Italian Flat Hearth Bread
    (Focaccia) 88
Herbed Mayonnaise 91

Italian Burgers 14
Italian Burgers with Confetti Salsa 43
Italian *Maionese* 91
Italian Sausage Burgers 63

Jeremiah Tower's Truffled Stars Burgers
    79
Jimmy Schmidt's Spicy Rattle Burgers
    with Chiles 76
Judy Rodgers' Zuni Burgers 72

Knecht Burgers 20
Korean Burgers 15
Kosher-Style Dill Pickles 88

Lamb Burgers, Hazelnut-Crusted 38
Lamb Burgers with Eggplant Salsa,
    Mustard-Grilled 36
Lamburgers à la Grecque with Cilantro-
    Mint Chutney 35
Loxburgers, Foxy 48

Matt Adams' Christy Hill Burgers 58
Mayonnaise 91
Mexican Burgers 15
Michael Chiarello's Italian Sausage
    Burgers 63
Middle Eastern Burgers 15
Mother's Pear Relish 90
Mushroom Burgers 15
Mu Shu Burgers 52
Mustard-Grilled Lamb Burgers with
    Eggplant Salsa 36
Mustard, China Moon Sesame 91

Napa Valley Basil-Smoked Burgers 32
New California Patty Melts 22
New York Burgers 15
Nut Burgers 28

Onion Burgers 15
Oslo Burgers 55

Pacific Island Burgers 15
Paul Prudhomme's Bronzed Burgers 65
Patty Melts, New California 22
Pear Relish, Mother's 90
Pickles, Bread-and-Butter 89
Pickles, Kosher-Style Dill 88

Relish, Buckeye Burger 90
Relish, Mother's Pear 90
Roasted Pepper Relish 41

INDEX TO CHEF AND RESTAURANT RECIPES

Salsa, Confetti 43
Salsa, Tropical Fruit 47
Sausage Burgers, Spicy 41
Sesame Mayonnaise 91
Sesame Mustard, China Moon 91
Southwestern Venison Burgers 71
Spicy Mayonnaise 91
Spicy Rattle Burgers with Chiles 76
Spicy Sausage Burgers with Roasted
    Pepper Relish 41
Spicy Tomato Catsup 92
Stephan Pyles's Southwestern Venison
    Burgers 71

Tangy Mayonnaise 91
Tart Cherry Catsup 92
Three-Nut Turkey Burgers with Tropical
    Fruit Salsa 47
Tomato Catsup, Spicy 92
Tomato Mayonnaise 91
Tropical Fruit Salsa 47
Truffled Burgers 79
Truffled Mayonnaise 91
Turkey Burgers, Cranberry-Glazed 27
Turkey Burgers, Three-Nut 47

Veal Burgers Cordon Bleu 61
Venison Burgers, Catahoula Parish 16
Venison Burgers, Southwestern 71
Vi Gianaras' Greek Panos' Burger 64

Whole-Wheat Hamburger Buns 86
Wonton Burgers 80

Zuni Burgers 72

Adams, Matt 58
Arcadia 75

Baby Routh 71, 87
Bix 66
Buckeye Roadhouse 66

Chez Panisse 82
Chiarello, Michael 63
China Moon Cafe 80
Christy Hill 58
Claiborne, Craig 61
Cocina 76

Fog City Diner 66

Gianaras, Vi 64
Goodfellow's 71

K-Paul's 65

Mustards Grill 66

Panos 64
Pawlcyn, Cindy 66
Prudhomme, Paul 65
Pyles, Stephan 71, 87

Rattlesnake Club 76
Rodgers, Judy 72
Rosenzweig, Anne 75
Roti 66
Routh Street Cafe 71, 87

Schmidt, Jimmy 76
Stars 79

Tejas 71
Tower, Jeremiah 79
Tra Vigne 63, 66
Tres Vita 76
Tropp, Barbara 80

Waters, Alice 82
Zuni Cafe 72

ALSO SEE *JAMES McNAIR'S BEEF COOKBOOK*:

Hamburgers 38
Spicy Ground Beef Patties 37

ACKNOWLEDGMENTS

All dishes have been provided by Dishes Delmar, San Francisco.

Most of the flatware is from Fillamento, San Francisco.

Glasses on the cover and pages 33 and 49 are from Out of Hand, San Francisco; page 17 is from Dishes Delmar; and pages 62 and 78 are from Fillamento.

Recipes were tested by
Ruth Dosher
Jan Ellis
Gail and Tad High
Dorothy Knecht
Bill and Naila Gallagher
Mary Ann Gilderbloom
Mark Gullikson
Connie Landry
Debbie Matsumoto
Meri McEneny
Lucille and J. O. McNair
Martha McNair
Maile Moore
John Richardson
Tom and Nancy Riess
Michele Sordi
Bob and Kristi Spence

To Chronicle Books for their continued support in all aspects of my career. Special thanks to Michelle Topolski for working with Sutter Home Winery to develop a special edition of the book for friends of Sutter Home.

To Bob Trinchero, Alex Morgan, and Stan Hock of Sutter Home Wines for putting together the great cookoff that was the impetus for this book. And to the Gold Group for involving me in the judging.

To Sharon Silva for another swift and superb round of editing my words.

To Cleve Gallat of CTA Graphics for putting together our nineteenth collaborative volume.

To John Carr for the generous loan of his home as test kitchen and photo studio, as well as for his constant friendship.

To Burt Tessler and James Wentworth for the use of dishes from their vintage Dishes Delmar collection.

To Ellen Berger-Quan for assisting with a few of the earlier photographs, including an early morning trip to the vineyards for fresh grapevines.

To Andrew Moore for his able assistance in the kitchen and the photo studio, as well as for helping me settle into my new Napa Valley home.

To my other friends and family who are always there for me, especially to Peter Baumgartner, Jan Ellis, Larry Heller, Louis Hicks, Gail and Tad High, Mark Leno, Marian and Alan May, Meri McEneny, J. O. and Lucille McNair, Martha and Devereux McNair, Jack Porter, John Richardson, Bob and Kristi Spence, and Felix Wiench.

To Beauregard Ezekiel Valentine, Joshua J. Chew, Michael T. Wigglebutt, and Dweasel Pickle for taste-testing so many burgers.